A Caring Mind

Matthew McKenzie

ISBN: 9798689567976

Dedicated to my dear mother

Rosemaire Mckenzie

Born 1955 – Died 2020

Reviews

"This book is truly the window and voice for all the hidden carers in society. I found it moving, informative and inspirational and being a carer myself made me realize that we're not alone". – Adella Hierons - Carer

"I found the book very moving". Kathryn Hill – Director for England at Carers Trust

"The book is a moving and powerful account of Matthew's experiences as a carer". Helen Hayes - Co-Chair of the APPG on Adult Social Care and the Labour MP for Dulwich & West Norwood

"In the beginning I felt I was reading Matthew's diary although with his permission it felt wrong, but understood his narrative. I now know Matthew's journey and as a carer also realise we all have our own experiences and communication is essential" - Lana Samuels - Carer

"Beautifully expressed and I found it very moving. I am sure it will be of great help to other Carers." - Jane Lyons – Involvement Lead for Croydon and Lewisham Adult Mental Health Services (SLaM)

I found it be a very interesting, touching and engaging read. There is so much that you have said that will resonate with many people and many very important areas of the carers experience are covered. To me, the book is a brilliant self-help guide. - Mark Foulds - Deputy CEO at Greenwich Carers Centre

"One word sums it up, and that word is" brilliant". I think you have written what most Carers want to say." – Kelvin Wheelan – Former Carer

"Matthew's candid account of his own painful experience as carer to his beloved mother was heartfelt and touching to read. It will resonate with many carers, including those who are possibly currently suffering in silence, and may encourage many to come forward and share their own experiences. " - Janice Walker - Carer Support Officer at Greenwich Carers Centre

"Matthew's account of his life as a carer is an inspiring and emotional read. Many unpaid carers will find it invaluable to support their own journey. This needs to be mandatory reading for all NHS and Social care staff". Peter Hasler - Former Nurse Director and Independent Mental Health Consultant.

"A very knowledgeable overview of the many different facets to caring; socially, politically, and culturally, with insightful references to mental health stigma." Paul Stewart - Carers Support Officer at Lewisham Carers Information

"As a fellow carer, I have identified with so many issues raised. It is an honest account of a very difficult situation. I recommend reading and sharing. In particular the thread running through the book that says, this could happen in any walk of life, at any time." – Faith Smith 'carer'

"I can see why you wrote it, and why you are so passionate about the carer role, and the need for a clear distinction between paid carers and the often unseen army of unpaid carers." - Prof Elizabeth Kuipers OBE

"A CARING MIND contains many heart-warming, life-affirming narratives you would expect from Mathew. Honest, pragmatic and calm - all elements he clearly used whilst caring for his Mum, who this book is dedicated too".- Catherine Gamble - Mental Health Professional Lead at The Royal College of Nursing

"Matthew's book is moving, honest, informative, practical, thought provoking and a privilege to read. This book has important messages for carers, professionals, advocacy organisations and policy makers." - Dr Ruth Allen CEO of British Association of Social Workers

"He has kept our IT running smoothly over many years. All the while he has been caring for his mother and supporting his brothers, but never bringing his disappointment or frustrations with the lack of support into the workplace. This book is testimony to the journey he has made and should be read by anyone who has the power to make a difference." Fiona Hamilton, Principal, London School of Osteopathy.

Contents

Telling your carer story

Welcome stranger. There are many books out there about caring for someone with mental illness. This book is my story about caring for my mother and also a way to raise awareness of unpaid carers. In my book there are terms I use, which I will define now. When I mean unpaid carers, I mean carers, who are caring for someone close to them, perhaps someone in the family or a very dear friend.

The term carer has been applied to many professions particularly those who care and support someone in the NHS. I certainly support all the brilliant work the NHS does especially during the current coronavirus pandemic, although I am aware there are those who are caring as well as working in the NHS, but we must remember that hidden away from society are those struggling to pick up the pieces left by the health and social care system. These people are unpaid carers and like me, anyone can become a carer one day. Either you will care for someone or be cared for yourself.

I also have noticed the word 'carer' used within the care worker profession, which we need to note: care workers are paid for the work they do while carers are doing their role out of love, duty or concern. It is true carers need financial benefits to help get by, but overall money is not the carers full concern unless in a focus to increase financial support.

This book will cover the following areas, the main part being my carer story. In Chapter 1 my book will point out why it is so important to tell your story if you are a carer. The next chapter will be about my story. Chapter 3 will discuss caring through coronavirus. Chapter 4 goes on to explore the profile of young carers, while chapter 5 will examine what I feel are the important carer characteristics. Chapter 6 will look at what helped me in my carer's journey and I hope that chapter gives ideas on what can help you if you are caring for someone.

In chapter 7, I look into carer networking, because I feel a carer should never have to cope by themselves and I also feel carers must stand together if they want to see positive change in their role and identity. Like any other marginalised group, carers have to learn to network together in order to make a difference.

Chapter 8 presents how I got involved co-production and my thoughts about involvement, I am not an expert in co-production and there are many complex processes to involve patients, service users and carers in shaping health and social care services. In that chapter I feel involvement in the NHS needs to be simple, but the problems of involving others are unfortunately complex.

Mental illness carries a lot of stigma and this can extend to the carer who is caring for someone suffering from it, chapter 9 looks at the causes of stigma and what could be done about it. There is also carer stigma, which can affect the caring role immensely.

The last chapter, being chapter 10 is a summing up of what I have learned through my carer's journey, although I am still a carer in some form as I step in to continue to form relations with my brothers, but as a veteran former carer I continue to advocate that unpaid carers have a place in society and should be protected in order to carry out their role because if the health and social care system fails the unpaid carer then that carer will be the next patient.

Who my book is aimed at

My book is mostly aimed at those who are caring or have cared for someone suffering from mental illness. When I mean mental illness I am referring to the following types of mental illness such as Anxiety disorders, Depression, bipolar, Eating disorders, Post-traumatic stress disorder or Psychotic disorders, including schizophrenia.

My mother developed a psychotic disorder around 2003 and although the illness made her condition vulnerable, she was still a very strong woman. She had to fight even harder for the things she held dear while suffering the illness, which eventually led to her suffering physical illness over the years.

My book is not only aimed at unpaid carers, below is a break down on who should also read this book.

Mental Health carers

Not all unpaid carers are the same, as I had mentioned earlier. When I refer to mental health carers, I am talking about a carer who is caring for someone with a mental illness. Mental health carers experience situations where the 'cared for' suffers a crisis in their mental illness and then after a while things may calm down, but the carer's loved one will not fully recover as before, while another crisis point looms in the distance.

This book's focus certainly is on mental health carers; however patients can also read this book to get an idea of what a carer might feel about the caring experience. Just a quick note, I often might refer the patient as 'cared for' as in being cared for by the carer or I will refer the patient as the carer's loved one as carers are often emotionally tied to who they are caring for.

Carer advocates and activists

The next type of people the book is aimed at is the carer advocates and carer activists. I would love to see more carers get the confidence and use their voice in the carer movement. We need more carers to network together and form a stronger sense of identity. Too often I have seen the angry carer drive others away and although there are a number of good reasons why a carer should be angry, it can do more damage to the carers' movement than anything else. I have seen angry carers lash out not only at the system, but at other carers as if to say they are suffering the most.

As with all groups struggling to find a voice in society, what carers need is solidarity. This cannot be achieved without the numbers of carers understanding each other and working with professionals in health and social care. I have watched how national carer charities like Carers UK and Carers Trust do over the years and I can see they have had some great successes, but a lot more needs to come from the army of carers – I think around 6.5 million in the UK alone.

I have been told I am sort of a carer activist and to some point I agree, although I did not realise it at the time. So I guess a big chunk of this book is coming from my carer activist hat, although I like to think of myself as developing carer peer support and showing examples of carer co-production and involvement. I like to think of myself as setting an example to other unpaid carers out there.

NHS professionals as a source of learning

The book is also aimed at mental health professionals and I have worked with many over the years.
In those years of NHS involvement as a carer, I have given many talks and speeches. I am not very good at speaking, but I am not afraid to get my ideas across.

This book is another way of getting my voice to the many NHS professionals out there. I cannot be everywhere, so I really hope my book can be shared across the NHS especially those who work at mental health trusts or in the mental health profession.

As mentioned before, I value the work that NHS professionals do, this also extends to the hard work social workers do. I think we can all learn from each other. I am also aware many professionals are carers themselves and I have come across NHS professionals who are also experts by experience due to suffering mental ill health. What I am trying to say is that identity is not always a black and white issue and we are all professionals in what we go through in life. I just hope we can continue to learn from each other. I want to avoid or limit the 'us vs them' attitude.

Leaders who shape services with policies

It is difficult to get an audience with those who lead on health and social care policies. These could be government ministers, CEOs of mental health trusts or even directors of nursing. This book can be useful to those who have found themselves leading on such policies, but who wonder about the experience of a mental health carer. This is vital because carers will end up using those very policies that were decided by such leaders.

Many carers by definition are silent about their experience and just end up coping in their role. A lot of carers can be quiet when someone powerful asks them about their experience of caring. So those deciding on policy can be hungry to find more sources of carer information. I hope this book provides that source of carer information and that although not everyone will agree what I have written, the book at least gets people to think about the role of mental health carers.

Why it is important to tell your story

When I started out as a carer caring not only for my mother, but also supporting in caring for my brothers, I was told to try and keep a journal. With a journal I can reflect back on what I did in my carer duties and how well things went. When you write down your experiences, it is easier to share them with others, but most of all telling your story greatly strengthens your identity.

Many carers out there suffer horribly and feel they just have to cope with it all. This could mean watching the person they care for succumb to illness. Other carers suffer by losing connections with family ties, while other carers suffer financial problems when the carer and 'cared for' might end up in the streets due to financial hardship. There are many ways carers can face problems, but worst of all is that carers can come to harm or their 'loved ones' can end up taking their own lives through suicide, this is not even half of what I have mentioned.

If more carers do not speak up about their experiences then how can we expect the system to accommodate us? How can we expect the carer movement to grow in strength? It should not be the aim of the carer to just simply cope and get on with it, but I do admit a lot of carers need encouragement and a way to develop confidence. I just hope carers find inspiration in my book and eventually tell their own story.

We can all learn from each other

This goes back to what I have mentioned in the section about the book also being aimed at health professionals. I sometimes think identities and labels can often get in the way of experiences. People are unique and special in their own right; we should try to avoid judging others unless we have walked in their shoes.

This can be common in any movement as sometimes people are quick to throw stones, probably because they have been failed by the community or by health and social care systems. I have experienced patients and service users attacking and calling out other patients because they feel that particular patient has not suffered enough to be classed as a mental health survivor. This can happen in carer circles as carers can quite easily turn on each other. We have all been through so much, even health professionals struggling with limited NHS resources. I do admit there are some bad eggs that spoil it for the rest of us, but those are few and far between.

There is so much we can learn from each other and it might be one of the only way forwards to develop a better experience for everyone, especially in co-production and involvement.

My story

Well here we are. It is time to tell my story, no matter how painful I may find it; I just hope others can learn from my story. If you are caring for someone suffering mental illness, then I definitely hope you can relate to my experience.

My story starts almost 18 years ago to this day. I have always imagined my mother to be a strong independent lady. She had a tough life and battled to raise four children, two of them with autism being unable to speak. My mother not only had a tough life, but a tough childhood. She had a happier time being raised by her grandmother over in Jamaica, but when she came to London to live with her mother things began to change for the worse.

Her mother became difficult to live with and suddenly her mother developed mental illness and unleashed violent tempers on my mother when she was young. This led to my mother living in supported housing in a society that was not welcoming to foreigners in the 1960s.

Fast forward to 2003 and I was working away from home in Basingstoke as a computer programmer.

Suddenly I remember getting a phone call from my sister who was living at home with our mother at the time. My sister was worried that our mother was behaving strangely. My sister mentioned that our mother was staying in her bed for days and not doing anything.

I traded ideas with my sister on what she could do and eventually my sister went to see the doctor in order to get a home visit. Without a full blown mental collapse, the GP did not see any emergency and I can only guess my mother hid her symptoms very well. With my sister's constant complaining that mother was not doing much around the house, my mother got fed up and asked my sister to live elsewhere. I got the feeling my sister was all too happy to live with her father, because without realising it, my sister was becoming a carer and certainly did not like it.

I kept in touch with my sister, but things were not easy for my sister as she was struggling to find work and also trying to find her place in the world. At the time I also continued to keep in touch with my mother and thought nothing else of what my sister mentioned or experienced. There was a worrying development as my two disabled brothers were left under my mother's care, while I was working away from home and my sister was living elsewhere.

Things begin to fall apart

Within a matter of weeks, I got another phone call from my sister that our mother was in hospital so the next day I travelled to London to find out what was going on. When I arrived at my mother's place, I was shocked to see broken glass at the front door, but I let myself in. The next morning I met with my sister and we took a trip to Ladywell inpatient Unit, which is a mental health inpatient unit run by South London & Maudsley NHS Foundation Trust.

I was not sure what to expect, it was a whole different experience for me, but when I stepped on to the ward, I was overwhelmed with other patients who were quite unwell. People were rushing around, but I do know that one of the mental health nurses was very kind and explained some procedures to me and my sister.

My heart sank when we visited my mother's room. Our mother certainly recognised us, but was very distraught. She kept asking the nurse as to why she was in hospital and she was not very well kempt. I noticed my mother's clothes were loose and my mother did not bother to dress, I certainly remembered looking into my mother's eyes. It was like there was no life in them.

I thought to myself this was not my mother, it couldn't be. All of the strong will had been zapped right out of her. I noticed how upset she was, but not crying at all as if there were no tears, but she was clearly upset and wanted to get out of there. I certainly noticed my sister took it harder than myself, I suspect my sister was going through a rough time with work and studies.

A couple more days after the visit to the hospital, I got another phone call from my mother's friend who mentioned that she had to let herself in the house to get my mother's belongings to take to the hospital, but had to smash the glass at the front door, which explained the broken glass. I also found out that both my brothers were put in temporary care, but the social worker felt one of my brothers should be put in supported housing.

I did not agree with the decision at the time, but looking back the social worker's view for my brother was instrumental because unfortunately the amount of times my mother ended up at the mental health unit was tragically numerous. Still my younger brother was in my mother's care for a very long length of time while I helped out.

There were many meetings on how to decide on my older brother's future and I strongly pressed that my brother should be a strong part of my mother's life, but stating this to my mother at times was difficult. The social worker around 2004 was very helpful and understanding, it is a shame there is a lack of social workers today, but years later to my horror I heard that the social worker that had helped my brother developed mental illness. I was sad to hear this and I am not sure what brought it on.

Over the years my mother struggled with her illness and we were eventually told she was suffering from a form of psychosis. It took a while for the clinicians to find out, and I remembered them asking us how our mother was before she was unwell. Looking back at the early years, I was glad they involved both my sister and me as carers. Though I did not know I was a carer at the time.

Over the years, my mother struggled with what seemed to be strange smells around the house, hearing voices although the voices were not as bad as the distrust my mother had for me. My mother would lash out at me and it was so sad to see over the years that distrust become stronger and more desperate.

When medication was not working, my mother would constantly be blaming me for intervening. Since there were times as a son that I would need to call my mother's social worker/care coordinator that my mother was relapsing. Some of the calls led to my mother being admitted to the mental health ward time and time again, but I was waiting for my mother to recover to begin the process of supporting her over and over again.

There often was a clash between me and the mental health professionals who would criticise me for trying to run my mother's life, but there was hardly any support or alternative than having me to step in. I am glad to say that some mental health professionals understood my position, while others took my mother's side. I did not care, all I wanted was for my mother's quality of life to improve, but at times confidentiality got in the way.

The start of my carer's journey

The first few months I was acting as a dutiful son to my mother, but around several months in I was told that I was a carer. It did not mean that much to me at the time, because I just kept trying to enhance the quality of life for my mother. I knew deep down inside somewhere beyond the mental illness that my mother appreciated the help. The sad fact was her mental illness saw me differently.

I had to keep intervening because sometimes the services could not react in time, especially when she had her other son living with us. I had to take on the role of looking after my brother while I was looking after my mother. I did not want my other brother to end up in care, although we had a very helpful foster carer who was ever so kind and understanding to us in the early years.

After several changes with my mother's medication, things began to settle down. We had a long period where my mother knew her condition and took anti-psychotic tablets. Those were the happiest times of being a carer and there was no problem of being involved. I even remembered the rare moment a care coordinator told us about planning for the future not just with a care plan, but with lasting power of attorney.

This was all to change when my mother stopped taking medication due to feeling she did not need medication anymore; the onset of the illness came back with vengeance and things were never the same after.

There were times that I just kept intervening to get my mother to hospital because I knew she could not cope in the community, I could clearly now recognise the signs as a mental health carer. I could remember the screams of fear and torment at night when my mother was battling the illness in her bedroom struggling to get to sleep. I would frantically ring for support because my mother could not cope.

I even remember stopping my mother from running out the house in the middle of the night in her bed clothes. Both my sister and myself phoned for a taxi to take our mother to another mental health trust which was NHS Oxleas, they were so kind, but both my sister and myself had to stay up from 11:00 pm at night till 7:00 am in the morning as our mother was transferred to a mental health unit closer to her location.

Our mother began to hate my sister and myself for stepping in, but I continued to care. The words from her stating we are not her children burn through me this very day. She was so unhappy that we kept taking her back to hospital to have a mental health assessment.

I knew what the risks were and if something terrible happened to my mother I felt I just could not live with myself. I had to step in because sometimes services were just not there to do it.

The Carer's Assessment

If not trying to be included in my mother's care plan, I often was given a carer's assessment. At first I thought the carers assessment was a waste of time, it felt I was being scrutinised. Eventually I changed my mind on the carer's assessment. This time I made such a fuss in order to get an assessment, because at least the carer's assessment helped plan what situations I may face as a carer. With carer's assessments back then they are usually provided by the mental health trust to see what things can aid you in providing care. Now the local authority is obligated to carry out carer's assessments under the Care Act 2014, although this might change under the COVID-19 Act, more on that later.

It was easier to get support from a carer's assessment before 2010, but after those years I think the assessment just became a form and nothing much else came of it. I have always mentioned to carers to request an assessment because even if not much comes out of the carer's assessment then at least it shows there are a need for them. Not everyone is going to like what I am going to say, but the council or local authority is pressured to save money, with carers refusing to being assessed then money can be saved, which is not always helpful for the unpaid carer struggling with providing care.

Carer's assessments can be linked to carer's rights especially if the assessment flags up breaches in the carer's rights. The more records of information kept by the NHS trust or local authority, the better off the carer is because no one can say they did not know of an impending problem a carer might face.

I still found some problems with carer's assessments overall as I felt that the way they were carried out was not very therapeutic. I felt carer's assessments should be a way to establish a relationship between the main carer and the care coordinator or at least NHS trust carer support officer. A big criticism psychiatry has often faced is that so much emphasis is on processes, pathways and systems and that not enough emphasis is on forming relations and connecting to the family dealing with mental health. Perhaps there is not enough staff, funds or maybe it's a culture problem at a specific NHS service. I felt sometimes things were rushed, but I do notice when a medical professional is either very skilled or empathic, while others just wanted the day to pass by.

Isolation over the years

As a carer I could not rely on carer financial benefits and I ended up finding a part time job working as IT support at the London School of Osteopathy. The job was perfect because I could continue to look after my mother and brother plus spend a day or two trying to make ends meet.

Over the years my work colleagues were kind and understanding about my caring situation, but there were times when an odd staff member ridiculed me as if they may never have had to care for someone themselves.

This can be common for the mental health carer as they often might want to keep their caring role a secret. Even from today's national mental health drive, so many people do not understand mental illness and some even think it is catching, you would not believe it. When mental illness strikes the family in the early stages, many of those who take on that caring role tend to keep quiet about it.

This was not limited to work friends, but general friends. I admit I did not have many friends myself, but I did see them dwindle away as they became busy with their own lives. I suspected some did not want to risk the experience of seeing my mother in a bad way and others felt she could be violent. I understood people and friends have to move on, but what I did not understand is that one or two older friends completely switched off and I never heard from them again.

I also noticed my mother lost many friends herself over the years. In fact no one really called her apart from bogus callers on the phone looking to take advantage of my mother's mental health. I remembered trying to speak to my mother to call her friends as a means of support only to realise that psychosis can zap a person's will to integrate with others. This can be down to what clinicians call the 'negative effects' of psychosis, which takes away things from someone's behaviour and even medication can add to that effect.

Often I would see my mother spend a lot of time watching TV and at first I thought she was just tired and lacking motivation, but looking back it certainly was her illness and the medication she was on made it difficult for her to be motivated. She often was very tired and there was a long periods where she still resorted to her bed. With all this tiredness and lack of drive, she began to put on physical weight.

There were two friends of my mother that continued to check in with her, but it was difficult for them, since they had to also deal with my mother's illness causing stress to their own family. Eventually I had to try to become not just a son and carer, but also a friend to my mother. I realised that I had to become many things to my mother filling in other roles in order to improve her quality of life, as I tried to be the carer, advocator, and son or even represent her at meetings.

I could not possibly do all those roles, since being a son and a friend clashed, I had to do things as a carer that would cause my mother to be angry, especially when her mental health deteriorated in a crisis. Even checking in to see if she was ok caused friction as my mother would get annoyed at me asking. It was only a matter of time before I retreated to my room to avoid the confrontation and pain of watching her suffer.

Caring during a difficult period

All of the intervening came to a head when my mother snapped when I had to step in again, she was relapsing into mental illness and I just could not get hold of her care coordinator. I rang, emailed and tried whatever I could, but in an emergency I ended up contacting social services who arranged for a quick mental health assessment for my mother. My mother was well enough to know I asked for her to be assessed, but in that one episode I knew her life was in danger and I had to step in again.

The medical professionals agreed after the assessment that my mother be sectioned again, it was the last straw and my mother's relationship changed towards me. During her last ward round she gave me a letter evicting me out of the house.

I remembered the meeting well and the care coordinator I spent ages trying to contact just sat in that ward round saying nothing. To make matters worse, a few weeks after, I got a call from the care coordinator thanking me for my support as if trying to get rid of me from providing care. Of course I had other ideas, she knew I was the main carer but thought since I am not living with my mother anymore then I am no long a carer.

Not many questions were asked as to how my mother felt she could cope on her own looking after her disabled son, but I did suspect at the time staff were under pressure. Somehow I had to make sure that while living elsewhere, I would still continue to check in with my mother and brother by visiting them.

In the back of my mind I knew when my mother was discharged after evicting me from her home that she still was quite unwell because she was angry and hateful towards me as she had felt that I conspired against her. I knew this was one of the effects of psychosis, but family counselling was limited as my mother kept refusing many forms of counselling or therapy.

Despite the pressure, I still kept to my role as carer and managed to find lodgings 20 minutes walking distance from the house. My mother was happy enough for me to visit, but she knew it was to check in on how she was coping. I just did not have faith in the services at the time to engage with my mother and I got the feeling that not all staff wanted to involve me. One good thing about the mental health service is I got supported by the carers support officer as I was allowed to attend the carers support group and I even eventually got more involved. Critically the local carers centre continued to support me, which was Carers Lewisham.

There were a few more mental health professionals that wanted to involve me, but the care coordinator was a different story. Maybe she was under a lot of pressure or just felt I was too much trouble. I was aware of increasing caseloads for social workers and care coordinators, but as a carer I would have thought that my intervention could help the social worker in her role.

South London & Maudsley provided excellent care coordinators in the past, I think overall I remember seven of them, but this one was the worst and the one after was her was not much better and even refused to give me a copy of my carer's assessment. The final care coordinator my mother had was very understanding and supportive even though he was under a lot of pressure.

There are issues with changes of mental health social workers, they are critical to understanding their client and family dynamics, with each new care coordinator there is a risk that they assume the patient's behaviour was never better than it currently is. There can be a lack of drive to push for recovery.

Making a difference

The whole experience of being failed by health and social care left me determined to make a difference and although some parts of the services were great, I noticed many holes where carers could fall through and end up being forgotten. I was often fearful about my future since I gave up so much in order to be there for my mother. I eventually became a carer governor for South London & Maudsley in order to provide a carer's insight at higher levels of involvement at a mental health trust. South London & Maudsley (I will call them SLaM for short) provides mental health services in the London boroughs of Lewisham, Southwark, Lambeth and Croydon.

As a carer's governor I stepped in to help the mental health trust improve services and raise the profile of mental health carers. I learned so much as a carer governor, but there was a lot of work to do and some things in the role I just did not understand since South London & Maudsley was a large organisation with many structures of mental health services.

In the back of my mind I wondered if families and carers understood their place in all these structures and I got further involved at SLaM in order to try and shape South London & Maudsley's services. I will talk more about my experience of involvement in another chapter, but for now I will continue with my story as a carer.

The family structure finally breaks down

When my mother was discharged before I got kicked out, I noticed although she was still quite unwell, she became even more tired and she put on so much weight, she struggled with caring for her son and each time I visited I saw my brother also put on weight. I became concerned and the harder I had tried to step in to support my brother the more my mother did not want me involved.

In desperation I had to contact social services who also knew what the outcome of the situation might be, but with my brother's physical health deteriorating along with my mother's health I put everything on the line. I wondered about my mother's medication, she was on medication before, but I wondered about the dosage, I had never seen her so tired and her mental illness was very prominent.

Since I was living elsewhere I could not care what my mother thought of me and arranged meetings with my brother's social worker team and tried to get the opinion of my brother's GP, but I had so many confidentiality problems. I reminded my mother to attend these important meetings to get some form support for her to care for her son, but my mother refused to attend: it was the mental illness again.

It was not long before my mother was admitted again and again to the hospital due to physical health problems, while still clinging on to her mental health. Social services had enough and although they asked me to take my brother away from my mother to another location, I just could not do it. I told them that they should arrange it themselves as I needed to continue some form of relationship with my mother somehow.

I remember checking in on my mother in the early morning after going for a jog. I let myself in only to see her sleeping on the sofa and the place in a mess. She did not notice me and my heart sank. I knew she was finally alone and isolated. I knew the family structure had broken down and with her being vulnerable I knew the outcomes would be terrible. My attention turned to supporting my mother the best way I could.

My brother ended up in care and this was one of the most painful times for me as I thought that I had failed to keep the family together. I visited my mother at the hospital, but she was still angry and distrustful of me due to the years of me intervening, which caused her to be sectioned under the mental health act. I could see she was suffering from respiratory problems not helped with her increasing weight.

She had difficulty breathing and I worried for her future. If there was one thing that I remembered as a carer for my mother it was the endless conversations I had with her to exercise and watch her weight; after a recent physical check-up my mother was told that she had developed diabetes. My mother often refused to acknowledge the condition and continued to eat unhealthily, but I knew again this was the mental health condition clouding my mother's mind.

Dealing with GPs and family counselling

I booked so many doctors' appointments that I am sure the doctors got fed up with me. Some doctors were very good and understood my role as a carer, while other GPs were confused as they were not sure how engage with mental health conversations with my mother. I remember one GP complaining about why I was arranging so many appointments due to my mother feeling so unwell all the time, but I had nowhere else to turn. If I did not raise the matter then it was my mother's physical health that would pay.

Dealing with health professionals made me become quite bitter at times because I felt I was put in the position of they always knew best, which was true for most of the part. As a carer such attitudes wore me down as I continued so see my mother's physical and mental health deteriorate even further.

While her other son was in care, we finally managed to agree to get family therapy and even my sister joined in the therapy sessions. I did not fully enjoy the sessions as I got the feeling I was to blame for my mother's feelings towards me.

I felt that mental health was being side tracked as an issue and more demands were put on me and my sister. There were times I felt the services were just too defensive about what they were providing and the excuse as to why my mother and I were at loggerheads was because I was told that I did not understand mental illness. Perhaps they were right to a point, I did not fully understand mental illness, but there can be no excuse for problems with services as well.

It is unfortunately common that some health professionals feel that families and carers can be seen as complainers. At the time I began running a carers forum and wanted other carers to get an idea of what family therapy was like and its potential, but I felt the service needed to be more developed.

Social care of my brothers

Over the years my mother's attitude changed as she realised that while both her sons were in care she became more isolated. It was clear that I was the only person visiting her apart from her care coordinator who saw her around once a month. I eventually moved back in with my mother, which was a relief for me since managing to hold down a job and caring back at home was easier than working, caring and living away from home. The worry and anxiety had been piling up on me for some time.

I still continued to improve the situation at home for my younger brother to come back, but this time it was very difficult. I felt social services treated my mother harshly and saw past incidents of her son against his mother. Since my younger brother could not speak, it was down to social services to speak on his behalf; with a new social worker set for my brother, I felt things were different compared to my brother's previous social workers.

With my mother's mental health not as sharp as it used to be, my mother was defenceless against certain accusations. I could clearly see that they blamed my mother more than the mental illness and without many minutes of meetings being sent I felt decisions were made to place her son in permanent care.

I cannot fully blame social services since my mother still did not want me fully involved to get her other son out of care, but this time without a social worker for my mother, there was no one to fight her corner. The mental health care coordinator did not want to get involved at that level and the fight was down to me.

There were times that I even felt social services did not want me to be part of my younger brother's life, but I got on very well with those who provided care and support for my older brother. They had known me the longest and knew that something was not quite right.

With this experience I know it must be awful when many lose their children to care because of mental illness. This goes especially for parents of younger carers (more on younger carers later).

Sometimes the family being split up might be the only way, but other times social services are too quick to split the family up and keep it that way. This could be due to the poor support given to those suffering mental illness and the lack of support for unpaid carers.

I fear for the future that coronavirus will make it difficult to continue a relationship with my brothers. I do hear from those who support my older brother and they even check in with me. I am very grateful for being included as a family member.

Carer's advocacy

If I said I had no support whatsoever then I would be lying. Over the years I have had a lot of support from my local Carers Centre, which was Carers Lewisham. This then extended to other carer centre support and I am very grateful for Carers Lambeth hub, but there are others, which I will get on to in a moment.

Basically a carer centre exists as a charity to provide support to carers, be it emotional support or providing advocacy, helping in that carer identity and building confidence and skills for unpaid carers. I have been a strong promoter of the carer centre and wish for them to continue.

There was many a difficult meeting where I had asked for a carers advocate to attend because I knew decisions would be made that would make it difficult to involve me. Some meetings were clinical and full of jargon, but back then Carers Lewisham had a mental health carer support officer who knew the mental health system and brought mental health carers together. I found some NHS staff complained about her, because she often stuck her nose in many carer problems.

If the carer support officer did not make her presence known, I am sure many families and carers' lives would have been very difficult. I also found the carer support officers from South London & Maudsley to be useful. I have known them for many years and I am still in contact with one of them. Carer support officers from mental health trusts 'especially in the community' are quite rare, but they have to deal with the most difficult cases.

The ones provided in Lewisham actually got me involved at the mental health trust in finding my voice as a carer. If there is one thing to say about South London & Maudsley is that their involvement for patients and carers is very good. When I mean involvement, I mean patients and carers get a chance to sign up to the trust involvement register and get involved in meetings, recruitment panels, training of health professionals, helping to develop policies and a whole lot more. Personally I think the acute sector of the NHS is still playing catch up when it comes to mental health trusts and involvement.

Patient and carer involvement will be critical for the future of the NHS because of how the coronavirus decimated the UK population. The public must get involved in health care, the public need to understand health care and be passionate about it.

Going back to carer advocacy, I also used the services of another charity, which was called Family Health ISIS. That charity specialised in providing support for the BAME (Black, Asian and Minority Ethnic) communities, particularly those from an Afro Caribbean background. Many BAME communities can be isolated and stigmatised when it comes to the mental health system. BAME groups can have a really hard time with mental health support and unfortunately studies and data show that BAME communities often get the worse kind of support.

Without the advocacy and support from Family Health ISIS, I am sure my mother's quality of life would have decreased even further. It was such a shame that Family Health ISIS funding got cut and we lost a vital community service since they existed for so many years.

In my mother's early years of her mental illness, she was so happy to be supported by Family Health ISIS, but in her later years she became more defensive and dismissive. I suspect that her mental health condition took its toll and medication did not help as much as it could. I strongly feel my mother suffered from mental health stigma with the mental illness clouding her judgement.

Overall if you are a carer, certainly consider finding carer advocacy in your area. If advocacy is not available it is under your carer rights to ask why carers have to cope by themselves.

The dreaded care plan

I have never had much of a good time with the patient care plan. These care plans are to involve the patient in planning their form of mental health recovery or at least coping with their mental illness. The problem with care plans is if the patient did not have much insight into their illness then they would never read too much into the care plan process.

Getting involved in care planning was tough since at times my mother did not want me involved and because of this, in the back of my mind I felt that this caused her to lose her life, which I will come to in a moment.

There are so many signs and opportunities to develop an excellent care plan, but it's a mistake to think that the care plan itself does the work. It must be a team effort and there has been really good care planning and also ones that were almost non-existent. I remember seeing one care plan provided to my mother with only a two page letter. Call it what you like, but it goes to show not much information could be pulled from it.

Without a doubt, I complained on behalf of my mother for the NHS staff to provide the full care plan and delve deep down into what underlying issues needed to be tackled. This could be any social support, physical health issues and especially tackling mental health issues or building up family relations.

There were times NHS staff were very good involving me in my mother's care plans, even when at times my mother did not want me involved, but most times my mother put up with me attending her care plan meetings.

I even arranged for her advocates to attend because my mother would always see me as her son and felt it was cheeky that I am almost telling her what to look out for. I would be more than happy for my mother to have a peer supporter help her, but there was a lack of peer supporters for service users and I felt the illness for my mother caused a lot of denial.

Changes in my mother's health

I did mention earlier on that my mother unfortunately passed away five months ago, leading to my writing of this book. I felt that there were times I could have stepped in more, but it was a fine balancing act to protect my own mental health and wellbeing as well as supporting my mother.

With the constant changes in medication and the worsening of mental illness, it finally took its toll on her. My mother's weight ballooned over the years and either she was too tired from medication or too unwell to know what was happening. My mother's final years were spent either being admitted to acute hospital services or the mental health ward. It was very painful to actually spend Christmas day at the mental health ward because she refused medication in the community and her mental health declined. I made it my effort to bring her older brother to visit her on the ward on Christmas back in 2019. The SLaM ward staff was exceptionally kind and wonderful that day and we even had Christmas dinner.

I felt she knew the medication was affecting her physical health and for her it was a fine line between coping with mental illness or a painful slow physical deterioration. I could see the changes in my mother and there was little I could do. I often pleaded with my mother to get a regular doctor's check-up, but in her last days she was so mentally unwell that she just did not trust me anymore and that was mainly the type of mental illness she had. She would not trust those who tried to help her, but looking back it was not her fault, it was sometimes lack of support or the illness being too difficult for her.

The day before she was admitted to hospital for the last time was when she called the police on me thinking I was trying to poison her, because she felt so physically unwell. The police were kind and understanding and sometimes I admit the police were not always sure how to deal with mental health cases although I feel some improvements have been made.

I told my mother that it was better to call the hospital than the police if she felt unwell since the police are not there to help in such circumstances, but I knew her mental health was deteriorating further.

The next morning she called for an ambulance to take her to hospital and in the space of two days her health declined rapidly. To be honest it was almost the beginning of the coronavirus pandemic and a lot of resources went to coronavirus patients. This time my mother was out of luck. The hospital spent a lot of time and effort tackling her physical health problems before then, but there was too much pressure on the health services this time.

On Thursday night my mother passed away and unfortunately they tried to call me, but ended up ringing my mother's own mobile instead of my phone. It hit me hard that I could not be with her during her last moments and I often wondered how she felt with her mental illness racing to torment her before her physical health dealt that final blow.

The only thing I felt reassured was that I told her the day before that I loved her, which many do not get the chance to tell their loved ones before something takes them away. However it was not the end as the cruel blow. My aunt was actually admitted to the same acute ward as my mother, in fact she was in the bed next to my mother, but she also passed away two weeks after my mother died.

I was shocked and distraught to lose two relations in such a short time, but it brought me closer to my other family relations.

A change in my identity from carer role model

As my mother passed away, I was at the cross roads. I could take the 18 years of knowledge as a carer activist and throw myself full time into work and earning a living. Or I could continue trying to make a difference in people's lives and develop my carer activism. I guess there was no comparison since I spent so long trying to improve the quality of my mother's life and involving my brothers in her life. This was partly the reason why I wrote this book, to tell my story, but during caring for my mother I gained a lot of confidence to speak up as an unpaid carer or a working carer since I was working part time.

Due to speaking at several conferences and debates as a carer, I felt it time to continue the networking with fellow carers from several carer centres. I wanted to continue to develop the carer forums and support groups. I enjoyed connecting with other carers who were going through similar experiences as I did.

Engaging with other carers developed my identity and made me feel I was not alone in the community. You could explain the carer's role to a friend or work colleague, but most carers just get what you are experiencing and this is some form of peer support. I am not saying that all carers understand the idea of peer support since I have come across carers who behave terribly to other carers. Some carers feel that they are suffering the most and point out that other carers are not caring if they do not suffer terribly. I have come across carers who are often angry at everyone and everything, which can be counterproductive and push people away from them.

Some carers feel they know it all while some carers push other carers out from being involved as if they are someone special. I think the thing I am trying to avoid is not using my skills to help other carers in their caring journey, which again is another reason I am writing this book.

I remember attending the leadership course at South London & Maudsley, which was championed by Kathryn Hill who was the carer lead for the trust at the time. I learned so much about making a difference. There were other things that helped develop my confidence and my role as a carer activist, but it was great that to be involved at the NHS trust at such a level. I managed to learn other things at South London & Maudsley foundation trust, but we will get into that in later chapters.

Caring through Coronavirus

At the time of me writing this book, I believe we have just been through the peak of the coronavirus, but unfortunately the virus is still out there and many people are nervous, worried and having to do the best they can in the most difficult situations.

When the coronavirus first arrived in the UK around late January, my mother was still around. She certainly was not in good health and with her pneumonia, diabetes and weight gain, I knew the outcome would not be good if she contracted the virus. In this chapter I discuss how the coronavirus affected my ability to provide care and I will also mention how the coronavirus placed extra problems on unpaid carers.

How coronavirus impacted my caring role

On and off during the later years of my caring journey, my mother was admitted to hospital several times not only for mental ill health, but her physical health was failing her. She knew recovery would be difficult and I knew it as well, but due to her ability to carry on she pulled through each time. Most times we got great support from the health and mental health services, but planning for her care was difficult, my mother knew her mental health medication was impacting her physical health over the years.

When the coronavirus eventually reached the UK I was in a state of worry and anxiety. I told my mother to keep an eye on the news to at least educate herself as to why people were trying to stockpile necessities. My worst fears were realised when my mother reported that there was nothing to worry about and that I was being fearful for no reason. I knew that was her mental illness talking. This was the first time I could relate to other mental health carers worrying about the coronavirus. How can you look after someone who is mentally struggling and keep them safe in a new dangerous world?

I stated my fears to my mother's social worker, but there was not much they could do. Mental health staff had to keep themselves safe as well, but it was not long before my mother ended up back in hospital, not because of the coronavirus but because her pneumonia came back again after a few weeks. Visiting my mother was difficult in hospital, because more and more patients were arriving with coronavirus infections, but I certainly remember my mother holding on and trying to respond to me while her mental illness flared up due to her anxiety.

One day at work, I got a call from Lewisham & Greenwich hospital trust. It was not good and I informed my line manager who kindly let me visit the hospital. On the bus ride to the hospital, I knew my worst fears had come to fruition, from that moment I was preparing myself for the worst.

The meeting with the doctors did not go well as even they were rushed to speak to me as if they were telling me there was not much they could do, but when I looked around I could see staff almost running around struggling with patients. When going into the hospital ward to see my mother, she was not making too much sense and I remember asking her if there was anything important that she wanted to tell me, with her words asking me to at least look after the house.

I helped to feed my mother at dinner time, but it was difficult for her where she was struggling to sit up and open her mouth to eat. At that point in time I had to say that I loved her, it was one of the most important things I have had to say in my life. It was such a shame my mother passed away around 64 years of age, which I felt is so young.

Over the years I have struggled to say how much I felt to my mother because I was pushed back by her mental illness lashing out at me. When I tried to show some form of affection to my mother, she became angry at how I allowed her to be admitted to the mental health ward or how I allowed her to be medicated. After a while of confrontation, I spent a lot of time in my room in order to avoid the arguments and accusations.

The other interesting thing is that I knew the acute ward was for mental health patients suffering physical ill health. I ended up finding some comfort from another carer visiting her sister at the time; we spoke for a long time to find some form of connection through a depressing scenario.
I told the carer what I did and what I knew about the health services, and she was intrigued and wanted to network with the other carers I knew. She was wondering why there was not a family and carer group at the hospital for people to share their experiences, but at that time with the coronavirus, I guess this would have been difficult.

The carer and I talked while leaving the hospital only to be told to get out of the way by other nurses. I could see a patient wrapped in what looked like silver wrapping being pulled along a patient trolley. My heart sank with fear as I knew this was a coronavirus victim. From then on I knew the hospital had become a battle zone.

Within the next day before my mother passed away I contacted my sister to visit our mother, so at least my sister could see her mother for what could be the last time. Something at the back of my mind was telling me this would be the last time and although I am not sure if there was some afterlife or anything spiritual, I just got that feeling to contact my sister.

The day before my mother passed away I was shocked to see my aunt in the next bed to my mother. I wondered what she was doing there and I greeted her and asked why she was in hospital. I just could not see the signs that my aunt was unwell, but my other aunt who was visiting her told me that she was in a much worse situation before.

The loss of my aunt

When my mother passed away, I was devastated because I felt I had failed my mother. Obviously it was not true for the 18 long years, I stepped in time and time again even when my mother did not want me involved, but again I knew it was the mental illness pushing everyone away. I knew if I did not intervene as a son and as a carer then my mother could have suffered far worse sooner.

In the back of my mind I felt that at least my mother was not suffering anymore and that I would not have to be anxious about the coronavirus infecting my mother. Little did I know that I was told that my aunt was transferred from the mental health ward to the acute ward several times due to ill health. I heard the inpatient ward had become infected with the coronavirus and two weeks after my mother passed away I got news that my aunt died. It was too early to say what took my aunt's life, but it must have been a multitude of things.

The news causing distress

Since trying to cope with my mother's and aunt's deaths, I was more intrigued on how badly the coronavirus was affecting the community. I wondered if the coronavirus was responsible for my aunt's death and that's when I found news about how the virus was affecting care homes.

The anxiety came back as I knew my brothers were in supported housing with groups of people. There was a risk their lives would be in danger. What is worse is that I could not visit them, but at least I could phone and be kept informed. I did let the people know that their mother had died, but it was sad they could not have visited her because of the coronavirus.

With the news becoming more depressing because of increasing deaths due to the coronavirus, I regulated my watching of the news. I followed the stats of infections and deaths on a public health website and used my carer forums to inform the carer members about the coronavirus. South London & Maudsley were excellent sending their staff to engage with the forums. We had the associate medical director in Lewisham to update on what they are doing to tackle the coronavirus and keep patients safe.

Over the following months speakers from the Patient Advice and Liaison service, psych liaison staff that worked with Lewisham Hospital, SLaM's Mental Health Act department and also Maudsley's complaints department engaged with my carers' forums. We had the mental health crisis café reporting back how they were dealing with clients and the modern matrons were linking in with my carer groups using virtual platforms to update us from the inpatient wards.

We were even joined at times by Lewisham and Greenwich hospital's mental health lead as before the coronavirus hit, we were planning some projects on involvement at those hospitals.

The impact on other carers

I knew that I would have to quickly keep in touch with carer members from those forums. Many carers were wondering how I managed to continue to run the forums two weeks after my mother passed away, but there were several reasons why I did this.

There was a risk that forums could die out if I could not muster the energy to continue them. I also felt carers needed to know what was happening with mental health services especially when services began to be locked down with some units being infected. Plus, with my mother's death, I just wanted to be useful to others and not mope around, I certainly did give time for myself to recuperate, but felt it would be easier to do something useful and make a difference.

I even managed to move my carers support group online with the help of Carers Greenwich. The mental health trust that covers Greenwich is Oxleas NHS mental health trust. Oxleas have been very supportive as I ran that carer support group. A lot of carers were in despair and needed that emotional support and connection.

With those forums I was hearing the fears and concerns from carer members. Many were worried about changes in emergency COVID-19 laws and how that impacted the 1983 Mental Health Act. Other carers were telling me how difficult it was to cope since patients were getting discharged sooner in order to free up beds for coronavirus patients.

Identity crisis

It was not long before I was back watching the news. Each day I was hearing the sacrifices from the hard-working nurses and NHS frontline staff. It was depressing to hear how the coronavirus was taking so many lives in the NHS, especially NHS workers from the BAME community. I remember that I kept looking at the statistics of coronavirus infections and scratching my head in frustration. I reported the statistics back to my carer forums to get responses from other carers.

We were wondering why the NHS the pride of the UK was getting hit so hard? What were the causes? Why were other countries health systems not struggling as much as in the UK? Carer members were also aware that some stats were inaccurate because each country's reporting system was different, but something with the UK infection and death statistics were not right.

It was not long before we heard about the 'clap for carers' campaign, where every Thursday night I saw many in the community give thanks to the NHS. They were right to do so because of the sacrifices made, but in the back of my mind there was this nagging feeling. I have been spending years trying to raise awareness of carers or unpaid carers and now I am not sure how to get the message across without upsetting people about who is actually a carer.

A lot of carers told me that such a campaign is needed and it would be best to tolerate the word 'carer', but many felt it did indeed blur the line between paid and unpaid carers. I had to get my message across somehow and with the support of the Royal College of Nursing, the British Association of Social Workers and the Royal College of Psychiatrists we ended up doing a set of webinars regarding connecting with carers during the COVID-19 crisis.

The webinars were very well attended online and I was grateful to the organisations for giving me that voice to speak on behalf of carers, especially those coping through the coronavirus pandemic. The RCN mental health lead Catherine Gamble had been very supportive over those months as I told her of my mother's passing. She continued to involve me in her work at South West London & St Georges on BAME nursing development and also in the RCN involvement for patients and carers.

Fear of the future

With the changes in emergency law to deal with the outbreak, the COVID-19 Bill had frightened many carers. The COVID-19 Bill was there to protect people, but one of the things under the COVID-19 Bill is that the Act temporarily suspends local authorities' legal duty to meet the care needs of all people who are eligible under the Care Act 2014.

Many carers still do not understand the Care Act 2014 and feel its presence is not far reaching. There was concern from carer forum members on how far the COVID-19 Bill would push back the Care Act, where the Care Act was designed to help unpaid carers.

The COVID-19 Act also weakens safeguards for detaining people under the Mental Health Act 1983 as this time only one doctor would be needed to sign off whether a person is sectioned. A lot of the BAME carer members were worried if this would increase the detention of those suffering mental distress from the BAME community since high levels of detention had already been carried out amongst them.

With the coronavirus outbreak a lot of carer centres had to close their buildings and move support online or via phone call. Added pressure was brought to bear on everyone and those who just coped in their caring role began to identify themselves as carers when the little support available began to dry up. With the furloughing of staff, some carers worried if support would ever be back to what it was before financial pressures hit the voluntary and charity sectors. Many community centres were lost during the austerity years and the coronavirus exploited the vulnerability in the community and possibly the NHS.

What next?

As the pandemic shows the figures of infections and deaths in the UK spiralled out of control. At the time of writing this book, it is far too early to tell what went right or wrong, we can only guess because this is a new virus that the UK was not fully prepared to deal with, but the UK dealt with the virus the best way it could.

The NHS did what it could in the best way possible, utilising the resources it had and carrying on despite the dangers and pressures the NHS frontline faced. The NHS now braces itself for another restructuring from the government and hopefully the NHS will get the support it deserves, but one might question how many restructures are needed to get things working?

With health and social care constantly being tested, unpaid carers and patients bear the brunt of weakening services. Many carers just fall silent when losing someone; they shrug their shoulders and carry on. Carers and their families need that support from their local carer centres to carry those silent voices and make them louder.

Too many have paid the ultimate price and are left to pick up the pieces. I am lucky enough to at least tell my story in other means and I even have a website and video channel online, while many carers have no avenue to let others witness their torment on how the coronavirus devastated their families, especially those who had to stand by and watch the virus wreak havoc on care homes and supported housing.

Unfortunate as it is, it certainly is the time for carers to band together and ask for that support while the UK is bracing itself for the second wave of coronavirus in 2020. Beyond 2020 it is anyone's guess on how far the coronavirus will go, but without research or more campaigning from the likes of Carers Trust, Carers UK or even the Royal College of Nursing and the British Association of Social Workers then the vulnerable will all pay the price.

The tragedy of Young carers

There are hidden voices even beyond unpaid carers; those voices are those of young carers, some I can guess are even as young as 5 years old. This chapter looks at the situation of young carers and how they can struggle to be heard. Of course there are many different types of carers, but young carers are at a certain disadvantage due to many factors and life experience can be one of the biggest against them.

I originally started out as a young carer, providing support for my older brother. My relationship with my brother was fairly happy; we were both mischievous in our younger days. I certainly did not class myself as a young carer, let alone even a carer but as usual my mother did most of the work, she loved all her children and would do anything for them.

If I did not have my parents around to help me out, I often wondered how my life would have turned out. Looking back I managed to have an ok education, met some friends and managed to take care of my own wellbeing, but what if the family structure is broken to begin with or if the support network is missing, then I can only guess I would have missed out on a lot of opportunities.

The prospects of young carers now

When I was a young carer, I can honestly say that I was fairly lucky and I must admit that I enjoyed supporting my brother although there were times when we struggled as a family. Now that I am examining the caring role, I have come across a few young carers and the horror stories that I have heard make me feel ashamed about how young carers can be treated.

If I take an example of a young carer who is caring for someone, perhaps a parent suffering mental ill health, I could say their prospects are not good. Most parents keep quiet about how bad their mental health is for fear of losing their child and means of support. This almost goes double for the young carer who is trying to protect the only family they know.

Young carers need that family structure because it is difficult for the community to step in. Many feel that the social care system has a difficult job to do in the first place. Younger carers not only have to worry about social care, they can be isolated from many systems, and they are even more likely to be bullied at school to the point that they end up truanting from school.

With the coronavirus spreading in the community the pressure on young carers has increased. Young carers got a lot of support from carer centres that provided young carer support and young carer support groups, but without such support then younger carers become isolated and unsure of who to reach out to.

If caring was not enough for younger carers to worry about then responsibility brought on by caring leads to young carers becoming stressed and anxious with so much on their shoulders. Some young carers are prone to mental ill health as they are not sure how to cope with difficult feelings especially feeling guilty or angry about how their 'cared for' relative is suffering. When you are an adult carer, you can at least research or find ways to reach out for emotional support.

Even if a young carer has the emotional strength, then there are challenges in dealing with someone else's emotions especially if a parent is suffering mental ill health.

As an adult carer looking after my mother, it was not always easy to deal with her emotions. I experienced anger, blame, stress and confusion from my mother. At best I knew how to deal with those emotions from her, I knew the triggers. At worst I had to keep my distance or be careful of what I did or said. Sometimes as a carer there were times when conflict came out of nowhere.

For a younger carer these mental health emotions can tear the family apart. It is difficult to provide care if you have had little to no life experience or training on caring for someone with mental ill health. Younger carers may end up even developing mental ill health as they struggle to find an outlet or cope with their caring role.

One thing I found difficult as a young person was coping with authority, although I found caring not much of a problem. I still experienced dealing with other people's moods a challenge, especially teachers. There was no mental health support in school, but back then I probably would have not even known what it meant. After providing care for many years, I can see the importance of providing emotional support in schools as young carers can be left to fend on their own. All this support either at the school or out in the community relies on funding. If no funding exists or is minimal then it is harder for young carers to get that vital support.

Worst of all if I found it difficult to cope with mental health or carer stigma, can you imagine someone the age of 9 trying to express their fears or embarrassment about their caring role? This is made worse if the young carer ends up being bullied; they will not open up to anyone, which is why young carer groups at those carer centres are so important. Such groups give young carers a chance to relate and strengthen their identity.

As I have mentioned before, carers just get what the caring experience is. Young people are still trying to understand their own identity and are thrown into a situation of discovering a carer's identity; if there is no reassurance then the young carer's outlet could be rage, depression and withdrawal.

Harder for young carers to network

As I write this book, I feel it is some form of activism as a way to get my point across. I have come across brave young carers who have developed the strength and skill to get heard. I even met a young carer following what I do at my carers support group, so she can develop a young carer's support group at Greenwich carers.

While I have managed to develop carer groups, speak at events and even help on co-production projects with the aim of raising the carer profile, the big reason I stepped forward to get involved was due to the disappointments I had with health and social care.

I am not saying health and social care failed me all the time, but when it did fail I certainly would try to make others know about it. With young carers I feel they are locked into the 'put up or shut up' situation. With life experience I could work out what could help carers all together by slowly chipping away at the system or services. Young carers do not have all these tools and may struggle to find that voice.

I am sure there are several young carer networks out there and I am sure there are spots of young carer co-production providing good practice, but I feel these are still few and far between. I have noticed campaigns from the national charity Carers Trust raising that young carers' voice, but there is still much to be done, especially during and after the coronavirus pandemic.

At least as a carer I had the freedom to network using many resources and technologies (see chapter 7) at my fingertips. I did a lot of research to target what could make the difference; I had to be brave a lot of times when attending meetings and get my point across. This is all so difficult for young carers who will have a tough time leading the way for themselves, they will need to be celebrated and more role models will be needed to break the stigma young carers face.

Without such support then young carers lives will continue to be tragic.

How on earth did I cope as a young carer?

Looking back after the years of caring for my mother, I wondered how on earth I managed to cope with supporting both my brothers especially when I was in my teens. It certainly helped that my mother was a very strong person and had to struggle on in order to care for all of us. She had a difficult marriage, but she struggled on even through all these difficulties.

I admit I did not have access to a young carers' network all those years ago and to be honest I felt this is the life that was dealt for me. Now looking back, I think young carers' support would have made so much difference for me. There would have been less strain on my parents because at times I often wondered why my father was angry and why my mother struggled with her marriage.

There were hidden signs that support could have made the difference, but I certainly remember how my mother clashed with social services on the support for her oldest son. My sister even mentioned to me that our mother became mentally unwell when our mother had to challenge social services again and again regarding the support for her other son. I felt my mother paid the ultimate price for caring for her children and even though I chipped in to provide support for my brothers, I felt compelled to step in again as my mother collapsed under the lack of support.

If all the above happened when I was much younger, I often wondered would I have paid that ultimate price as a younger carer. Would I have collapsed under the mental strain and be another statistic as a young carer?

Carer traits and characteristics

When people think about unpaid carers, they often think that the person is just caring for someone. In a way they are correct, but delve a little deeper and they could be off target. There is a whole lot more to a carer's world than what people might think.

So I have decided to list and briefly explain some unpaid character traits, this chapter is aimed not only at health professionals, but carers themselves who might wish to understand what they might find helpful on their carers journey.

Please take note, not all unpaid carers are the same and due to trying to keep this chapter short, I have missed out a lot of carer character traits and skills.

Providing a simple hug

Not all carers can do this; it really depends on how the relationship is developing with the 'cared for'. Some unpaid carers are very close to the person suffering either mental or physical ill health, but giving a simple hug to that person can help more than any words can say. I myself have tried this and sometimes it works and other times I was pushed away. As a carer, if pushed away please do not take it to heart; remember mental illness is probably not the person you see before you.

Authenticity

Just caring for someone shows that you are wearing that carer's badge, no one can say you have not been there. If asked to speak about your carer's journey, then you will understand. An unpaid carer's journey can be difficult, full of tension and almost a roller coaster ride. As a carer you can expect to take some massive blows, but at the same time you are growing stronger in your cause.

Being a shoulder to cry on

Not always easy especially if the 'cared for' is distant from you, but as a carer you can always be there as a shoulder to cry on. There will be times that the 'cared for' will be let down by everyone, be it friends, health services and so on. If you are close to the 'cared for', just being a carer will give you the opportunity to be the last person they can cry to. Isolation and loneliness are common with those suffering severe mental illness, being there for them can make a big difference.

Being Present

This is one of the most important traits of an unpaid carer. There are many ways to provide care, but being there is the ultimate role of a carer. Some people have big families, but not everyone in that family is going to equally care for that person. There will usually be the main carer doing that role.

Sometimes the carer is the one who will sacrifice or put on hold their life to provide that much needed support. A carer will be there at hospital appointments, doctor's appointments, care plan assessments, benefit assessments; they will provide medication or chase things up and more. Being there for the 'cared for' is what it takes to be a carer.

Being there when times are tough

Being there is of course NOT enough; it is being there when the chips are down that is when the true worth of being a carer is shown – when everything is on the line. It is also ok to provide support when the crisis is over and I am aware that carers cannot be around the person all the time.

I am also aware that it is not a criticism of carers who tried so hard, but were pushed away, especially mental health carers. Still, there will be times when the impossible may be asked of you, as a carer you will need to be there especially during a crisis.

Believing

There are not many rule books on being a carer. There have been times when I have thought to myself, am I doing the right thing, because no one can really tell you that you are living your life the best way.

There were times my 'cared for' hit crisis after crisis and I was banging my head against a brick wall with all the bureaucracy, confidentiality and red tape. I was even dealing with bullying from NHS staff siding with the 'cared for's' criticism of me and to be frank, I was on my own.

The keyword is 'Belief', you as a carer might have to dig deep down and start believing in yourself. What are you caring for? What are you fighting for? What are the costs? The sacrifices? Is it all your fault? Sometimes only you can answer those questions.

Caring can be a very lonely journey at times.

Compassion

Compassion is very close to being there as a carer, you will need to show compassion, patience and to be kind. It is not easy to do this if you are under stress or constant pressure. Just being compassionate can even extend to others if you practice being compassionate to the person you care for. If you lack compassion, then you could do damage to the caring role and even your relationship to the person you are caring for.

Confidentiality

Sometimes carers need to keep the confidentiality of the person care for, but most times a carer will have to deal with 'confidentiality'. It is frustrating because in the end it will be you that is providing the care and support, but how can you do your role if no one is saying what to expect when caring for the 'cared for'?

It's like they are saying 'Just get on with it', when the patient is discharged into your care. I have noticed a culture where health professionals state the 'cared for' is discharged to the social worker's care or the care coordinator's care, but what happens they move on from their jobs or leave? The carer is the constant person in that role and should never be pushed aside or forgotten. Learn how confidentiality works, especially when Carers Rights Day takes place each year. Certainly read up on the NHS trusts' confidentiality booklets or leaflets; ask for them if they are not present.

Connection

Being a connection to someone is not easy at all. It depends how close you are to the 'cared for'. Sometimes a carer is just a person in name and role, but being a connection to someone is highly psychological. There are whole books on the subject of connecting to others and one of the methods is the '5 ways of wellbeing'.

It is not always easy connecting to someone who is unwell, but it can benefit yourself as well as the 'cared for'.

Empathy

Similar to compassion, empathy is the capacity to understand or feel what the 'cared for' is experiencing. This is why many carers try hard to work out what the situation is, so that they can provide adequate care and support. Without empathy then you are relying on guess work, but sometimes it is not always the carer's fault.

If unpaid carers are pushed out due to confidentiality or not involved, it is difficult to understand what the person is going through, especially if it's mental health. Remember, if the health professional is not always present and the 'cared for' is very unwell, then it is usually up to the unpaid carer be it friend, neighbour or relation to try and be empathic.

Helping

Sometimes caring is a grey area, there is more to caring than just helping with physical or mental health support. It is also being around to help, this might be arranging meetings, advocating, helping the health professional, helping with money situations and so on.

Hope

Without this trait, you might even want to give up on caring for someone; there needs to be some form of hope that the 'cared for' will recover or at least live on with the illness. Sometimes unfortunately there is no recovery, so all you can do is hope and be a witness to the person's suffering, but deep down inside all unpaid carers hope for some change. As with my mother, I followed her journey to the end as almost a witness, so she was never truly walking alone. It was painful to watch the slow deterioration, but there was always hope.

Love

Another common trait with all unpaid carers is that you care because you love the person or are emotionally tied to them. Love is a vague word, but without some form of love, it is difficult to care for someone let alone care for anything.

Sometimes people overlook the love between carer and 'cared for', but it is there. Even if the carer had to walk away from their role, this still could be done out of love and when things really go wrong. This is sometimes why they say love hurts.

Loyalty

Very difficult for carers to do, being loyal to the 'cared for' can be an important trait, but what happens when the 'cared for' refuses help? When does the question of being loyal become a risk? This is when carers need to break confidentiality and raise the issue if the 'cared for' is at severe risk. A good example is updating the doctor, social worker or another professional.

Open and loving friends

Not really a carer trait, but something a carer could find helpful. Unfortunately, friends tend to go packing when having to deal with a carer who is fighting something depressing. It does not help that carers end up lacking a social life, so it is harder to make new friends.

If you are lucky to have friends around who are open and understanding, it can help you in your carer journey to never walk alone, but expect that other carers will be your friends, because they just get it.

Openness

A risky trait, but expect to use it sometimes. As a carer you will have to be honest about a situation, you might expect to be put between a rock and a hard place. When the 'cared for' is refusing help, you will have to raise the call for help, even against the 'cared for's' wishes. A carer will have to be truthful and open about what is going wrong and expect your relationship with the 'cared for' to decline, but think to yourself, what is the risk? You might be thankful one day that you were open and honest about something. Expect the relationship to be slow to build back up again, if ever.

Phone call to check on how someone is

As a carer, it helps to use the many tools in your carer's journey; this is often necessary if you are caring from a distance. Even if the 'cared for' is not in crisis, a carer might call to see how things are, you never know what the 'cared for' might say. Take note, that with the advent of smart phones, it might help to add the person on WhatsApp, Skype, Facebook or other applications. Due to the coronavirus this is more critical than ever.

Quality time

Sometimes it is not always about care, more care and caring. Spending quality time with the person can help make a difference. Think of it this way, what was the person like before they became unwell? Your relationship might have changed somewhat, but deep down they are still that same person. Sometimes spending quality time is what is needed and expect to do this as a carer to help connect with them. There were times I played board games with my mother or enjoyed poetry with her when I ran a computer class for service users.

Safety

Did I say this is common among carers? It probably is the number one rule for unpaid carers. You might think providing a safe space for the 'cared for' is all that it is, but that is not the full story. Ever heard of the consequences when things go wrong in the health system? Carers will sometimes protect the 'cared for' especially when serious incidents will occur, think of wrong medications provided, or wrong decisions putting the 'cared for' at risk.

It can be a tug of war when the carer has to push for the 'cared for' to get that support from the health and social care system. Overall the carer will have to be a shield for many things and expect to take some blows.

Showing up physically and mentally

Not the same as being there, expect to take on health and social care settings. Sometimes you as a carer might think some things are being done as a tick box, well you could be right. As a carer you will have to deal with the following professionals.

- Clinical Psychologist

- Psychiatrist
- Nurses (different Bands)
- Mental Health Counsellor (families)
- Social Worker
- Care Coordinator
- Ward Pharmacist
- Occupational Therapist
- Ward Manager
- Admin for services
- GP
- Peer Specialists
- Advocates
- PALS Team
- Home Treatment team staff

Yep! and this is only the HALF of it. So as a carer how would you prepare for an important meeting, if you are not sure what that person does or if the professional is being difficult? Well, I am sure at some point I will write about engaging with professionals, but as a carer do not expect the 'cared for' to do the legwork, especially if they are very unwell.

With the many types of professionals in the system, this was one of the reasons why I started carer forums so roles could be explained and sometimes monitored on how carer awareness was progressing.

Smiling or trying to smile

As a carer you don't have to do this, in fact it is better to seek support if you are feeling down rather than pretend and put on a false smile. It does obviously help to keep one's spirits up, but it is important to be honest with your wellbeing and reach out for support for yourself as well. It is vital you find your local carers' centre and check in with them.

Someone to really listen

This is very important for unpaid carers. If the 'cared for' has no one to talk to then expect to listen and avoid saying much or criticising. This is not something that is easy to do, because it depends on your relationship with the 'cared for'.

There have been times that I have had to listen because the person I cared for ended up ranting due to being unhappy with how she was treated. It was just because there was no one she would trust to rant to instead, not even the Samaritans. In the end, I just kept quiet and listened, then walked away hoping that her complaining helped in some way. As a carer expect to listen, but also expect to learn some listening skills.

Time alone

It is so important that you as a carer get time alone for yourself; it might be for recharging your energies, thinking things through or just relaxing. This is because a carer has to go through a lot, especially all the things that can play on the carer's mind. If a carer cannot get time alone, then they could themselves become the next patient.

Trust

In health professionals we trust!

As a carer you will need to put your trust in professionals because you cannot do everything yourself. You will have to hope and trust that your doctor will involve you in the 'cared for' situation. If that does not work, then pray the doctor is skilled in being diplomatic enough to remind the patient why they need support from those close to them.

Sometimes doctors tend to take the easy way out and let the patient's word be law, but life is not always as simple as that Why? Think about those serious incidents when carers or public were right about someone being at risk and the health professionals were wrong.

It does happen and unfortunately it will happen again, but until then the carer will have to trust in others and trust the 'cared for' will seek support. If that does not work then certainly choose another professional as it is your right to get someone who is holistic.

Words of encouragement

Expect as a carer to encourage the 'cared for' to not give up hope. The carer will need to be skilled in being supportive with words and not only just in listening skills. In fact a carer may end up becoming some form of counsellor for the 'cared for'. I once took a course called 'Coaching Conversational Skills for Carers' introduced by carer Roger Oliver which I found quite useful.

The conclusion

Unfortunately these are just some of the carer's traits in the carer's journey. The carers world can be a difficult long struggle, but it can also be rewarding as you share the 'cared for's' life successes, hopes, dreams and struggles. It need not be unbearably tough if you try to learn as much as you can about what it means to be a carer.

What I found vital for carer support

Over the years I needed support as a carer in order to care for my mother, but also needed to care for myself. I eventually developed my role as a carer activist, but if I could not get any support then I often would question what on earth I was doing.

There have been times when things got so bad on my carer's journey that I would not know where to turn, but looking back I am glad I managed to get some support and insight into my caring role.

Below are some tips about what helped me.

Carer advocacy

I want to mention carer advocacy first because it was one of the first things I tended to use as a carer. I managed to get a lot of carer advocacy from my local carers' centre, Carers Lewisham. The carer advocate attended important meetings about my mother. At those meetings a lot of clinical jargon was used and my carer's advocate was kind enough to break things down for me.

Carers Lewisham also provided carers support groups as did South London & Maudsley. I found both carer support groups to be very helpful. When it came to form filling, the carer advocate also helped by going through my carer's assessment or developing a care plan for me.

I also got carer's advocacy from an organisation called 'Family Health ISIS', which was a BME community group charity. BME as meaning Black and Minority Ethnic.

They were very helpful with supporting my mother and myself and supported me when I developed a computer skills workshop for service users. The organisation even helped develop my BME carers forum

Peer support for my mother

Getting support for yourself as a carer is only half of it, as a carer you do need support for the person you care for. For a mental health carer this usually comes from a doctor, mental health services and so on. Each support you can get is different depending on the need. The support my mother was referred to was a BME charity which provided a sense of identity from a BME perspective and also a way to cope with mental ill health.

BAME communities can suffer double the stigma because society can discriminate against them which can lead to them becoming mentally unwell, and if they do end up suffering mental illness then society can also discriminate against illness as well.

I have experienced how my mother suffered mental health discrimination not just from those outside mental health services, but within them and from BAME staff. It was noted at discussions with BAME support groups that even some BME staff can be tokenistic in a mental health setting. It has been noted a few BAME staff may not provide the much needed care and support to BME service users.

I am certainly for more BAME NHS staff reaching the heights of leadership and success, but being BAME is not enough in itself. Over the years I found out that you cannot always teach a person to care for someone and skills can only get a professional so far. Still I notice NHS services continuing to work on developing a caring mental health staff, which is always a good thing.

Carer involvement in health and social care

I tend to notice the more carers complain about the service, the more things stay the same. If you want to change something then it is best to get involved. Even if you do not fully understand what you are doing, there is something about developing services with that carers, touch. It was 5 years into my caring journey when I finally got involved in telling my story. I value the involvement of patients and carers in the NHS because it shows that the NHS values those who use their services.

Carers of course do not have to get involved in shaping services as they have a lot to deal with. Some carers even really do have such a bad time with services that they just want to steer clear of them. I guess it is the carer's right, but I feel we have to burn the candle at both ends and try and make a difference. The carer involvement culture has a long way to go, but things are moving forward.

My Path to carer involvement

I have had a long and adventurous involvement journey. I am still involved in quite a lot of carer projects either at mental health trusts or out in the community. Once you get involved in shaping services then you never look back, it can be a fulfilling experience.

- Carer Centre events

My first form of involvement was through my local carers' centre. I got involved by just telling my story when health professionals attended training classes regarding identifying carers. The Carer Centre staff provided many a platform for me to tell my story.

- SLaM involvement

I also told my story at the South London & Maudsley carers' listening event and there must have been an audience of 200 where I was scared out of my wits. I was very grateful for being given the opportunity to share my story and to be honest my story was not always pleasant because there are things that health professionals just did not want to hear, but my story can always be a good learning experience.

After developing the confidence to speak about my carer's journey, I was sponsored by SLaM's carers support officers to join the Maudsley's involvement register. The involvement register allows patients and carers to help shape services by attending meetings, having a say on policies and processes, being valued as experts by experience and taking part in job interview panels. The SLaM involvement register is rich with opportunities on learning about the mental health profession as many view mental health as being a top down take it or leave it service structure. Being involved can really make a difference.

SLaM is blessed with patient and public involvement leads being Alice Glover and Jane Lyons who have been very helpful in supporting my carer groups and forums.

- Service User Involvement in Training & Education

The South London & Maudsley trust has many sub groups and projects on involvement. One of the projects is SUITE, which stands for Service User Involvement in Training and Education. SUITE has been around for quite a long time and I have been involved in training mental health staff on and off while being a SUITE member.

The team consist of carers and service users where I have developed a lot of skills regarding training of NHS staff. Some of the skills I used when speaking at the National Mental Health Nurses director forum where I was invited by Professor Hilary McCallion CBE, Peter Hasler and Mel Coombs who was director of Nursing at Cambridge and Peterborough NHS Foundation Trust at the time.

I found SUITE to be invaluable in learning the ropes on getting involved in educating mental health professionals. The training facilitator of the project Angela Mitchell provided a lot of inspiration in an often challenging setting. I guess I could write a whole book about what I learned at SUITE, but maybe that is for another day.

- SLaM carer governor

It must have been around 2013 when I became a carer governor for SLaM. I think there must be a video of me speaking about being a SLaM carer governor on the Maudsley's YouTube channel. I am very proud of it.

I was also very proud in being a carer governor; although I only served a 3-year term I learned a lot about working in partnership with the NHS trust and especially about the importance of community. I must admit looking back I was under a lot of strain in my caring role as a governor, but I managed to pull through and the SLaM senior staff was always welcoming and supportive.

I felt SLaM gave me a lot of attention and celebrated my carer's voice often. I do admit there were times when I got things wrong and there were times I should have done more, maybe I am being too apologetic, I do not know.

I often remember how my fellow SLaM governors supported me, some were of course very competitive, but in such a role it is almost expected. If you as a carer ever get a chance to go for being an NHS governor it is worth the time, but it can also be hard work.

- West London NHS Trust involvement

I have always told carers to network and go check how other mental health or carer services are running. It was not long before I got involved over in west London through a community mental health charity called We-Coproduce. The energy and direction of We-Coproduce was fantastic and all the time Jane McGrath who is the CEO of We-Coproduce invited me to coproduce as much as possible especially when it comes to how West London NHS Trust engages with families and carers.

It was not long before I got involved in West London NHS Trust. I found staff there very enthusiastic, friendly and welcoming. If there was anything to say about West London NHS Trust, I admit the staff members are very proud of what they do. I am sure of course it depends on your experience of services with mental health trusts.

There were many health professionals who made an impression on me at that trust, but one who did stand out was Gillian Kelly who was the Deputy Director of Nursing at the time. She often had a lot of time for me in a very challenging role.

- Oxleas NHS family and carer meeting

I cannot even remember how I got involved at Oxleas Mental Health Trust, although my mother used their services so it was only fair to give my carer views. I was brought on board by Oxleas NHS carers lead Anna Chan who many carers at my groups remember. I am sure they miss her and talk about Anna often.

Oxleas have been very supportive of the work I do as a carer peer role model. My very first carer peer support group was set up over in the Royal Borough of Greenwich, although my other carer forums have existed for a long time in the other boroughs.

I found running a carer peer support group to be a completely different experience due to forming a deeper connection with carers. If it was not for the carers' centre Greenwich Carers it would have been so difficult to set up such a group.

Being recognised as a carer

Moving away from involvement, being recognised as a carer made a lot of difference in my life. If I had not been recognised as a carer, there would have been a small chance that I would walk away from caring for my mother. It is vital as a carer you can get that carers assessment and be recorded as the main carer or be offered carer support.

I must admit there were times when I felt I was being pushed away as a carer, but luckily this was not often and I feel unfortunately it is part of that carer's journey; there will be times when the pressure is too much that people just snap. Still as carers we usually put up with it and move on, but looking back it is important carers pluck up the courage to complain.

The reason for the title unpaid carer is that we are unpaid to provide care and support. The system is not perfect and many carers will fall through the cracks, but we should not be constantly blamed as for each carer the scenario is different.

Carer policy

Both Carers UK and Carers Trust are national charities that strongly advocate for the carer's rights and welfare. I often see carer surveys online or via my email asking for my opinion on care and my experience of caring. I strongly urge carers not to ignore these surveys as they help shape decisions and develop policies. I know some carers will find it boring filling in surveys and questionnaires, but think back to the time you were let down by services. Such experiences should drive you on, but I agree change can at times be slow for carers.

- Carers UK

If there is anything I enjoy about Carers UK it would be their Annual General Meetings. It is a chance to network with carers like no other event. Carers UK have had a lot of success over the years influencing change and carer policies, but as with everything there is so much to do. I have been involved with Carers UK for quite a while and relished the spotlight when I talked at their 2019 AGM. It really should be a carer's dream to have your caring journey recognised be it a good or bad journey. Life can be so short, so it is important we leave a statement behind.

- Carers Trust

I have also been involved in Carers Trust especially on their carer's Triangle of Care policy, which was developed by carer Alan Worthington. Alan has been instrumental in influencing, strengthening and holding to account mental health trusts when it comes to improving outcomes for carers.

I ended up being part of this wonderful drive to make a difference for mental health carers by being part of the Triangle of Care national steering group. I admired how Ruth Hannan the policy and mental health manager at Carers Trust had so much energy for carers. She worked so hard in driving the Triangle of Care Scheme.

One thing I remembered about Ruth was that red dress she often wore as I felt it symbolised energy while to others especially stubborn mental health trusts it probably symbolised danger. Ruth incorporated many carers into making a difference in their lives and making a change.

Carer activism and taking the lead

From being involved on the Triangle of Care scheme, I developed a stronger sense of carer activism. There was a change from sitting on the sides to being determined. There was no shame if things did not work out because you would just keep trying again to make a change, but find another way do it.

I now see it vital that carers learn a bit about activism and especially observe how other marginalised groups do it. I feel the carer movement has come a long way, but carers should not rest on the side lines and only complain. Carers need to try to get involved and be counted; I feel at times carers should try and take the lead, but they need a lot of confidence.

The formation of carer groups

With the added strength of carer activism that I picked up by being involved in the Triangle of Care, I incorporated that skill into my carer groups. My carer forums were designed to give carers a greater chance to understand how the mental health services work; they were not carer support groups because carers do not have much time to tell their story if at all.

I started my first carer forum in the London borough Lewisham, then set up another with Carers Hub Lambeth and then developed a BAME carers forum back in Lewisham, and the last forum I built was for the London borough of Southwark. After many years I realised that carer support groups could strengthen the forums as many carers tend to connect first and then develop an interest in mental health services. I then worked to run a carer peer support group in Greenwich and to develop another one for the borough of Merton with another carer.

As a carer I often get told that carer support groups are running in an area already, but with hundreds of carers in an area, I am surprised to see only a few turn up in a group. I have mentioned that carer peer support groups give confidence to carers to network and link up with each other. The more carer groups the better as carers begin to look out for each other. I think it is about setting an example, but being a peer role model can be very challenging as you could come across a carer who wants change and wants it now.

Running carer forums can sometimes be difficult since a lot of chasing is required to get information and updates. I am also grateful for those who did attend and support the forum. A special thanks goes to Helen Hayes Member of Parliament for Dulwich and West Norwood and also co-chair of All Party Parliament Group on Adult Social Care. Helen attended not only a carer forum in one borough, but also in another and for a very long time. In the past other MPs have attended including my own MP Janet Daby and MP Neil Coyle who are both carers themselves.

Healthwatch

It was only a matter of time before I got a lot of support from community organisations called Healthwatch. Healthwatch is an independent national champion for people who use health and social care services.

There is a Healthwatch in each of the London boroughs or regions around the country and the ones that engaged with my groups were usually Healthwatch Lewisham, Healthwatch Lambeth, Healthwatch Southwark, Healthwatch Bromley and Healthwatch Greenwich.

I found the staff at Healthwatch spent a lot of time getting views about health and social care from the groups as carers became more knowledgeable about services over the years. I am sure some staff at Healthwatch was amazed about how much those carers knew.

Royal College of Nursing

When the Triangle of Care policy was moving on from Carers Trust, it ended up back with the Royal College of Nursing which is the largest nursing union and professional body in the world; with the UK's proud history of nursing it was a privilege to be involved with the Royal College of Nursing as a carer member.

The RCN lead for Mental Health and Education Catherine Gamble supported me every step of the way, I am not sure how she manages to do so many roles, but she is filled with dedication and passion when it comes to nursing.

NHS Trusts

It was not only mental health trusts that I got involved in or tried to engage with. I got a lot of support from Guys and St Thomas NHS Trust and Kings College Hospital. There are of course strong links between mental and physical health and my mother used the services of acute as well as psychiatric hospitals. My mother unfortunately paid the price with both physical and mental health declining; I feel it is something Kings Health Partners needs to continue to pay attention to – the life mortality rate, which is a shocking 20-year loss for mental health patients.

I felt it important that such NHS trusts work towards involving mental health carers. I feel the culture of acute hospitals compared to mental health hospitals is quite different in engagement and involvement, I am not sure why as yet, and I do feel a lot of work needs to be done to give families, patients and carers a greater say in those services.

Despite my views I noticed so many in the NHS working hard to keep the focus on carers. Sorry if I cannot mention everyone, but with my involvement at NHS England and Improvement, I can see they are strengthening their commitment to carers. I have watched Jen Kenward who is NHS England and Improvement experience of care lead. I can fully say that Jen is committed to carers and she is often very knowledgeable.

I can only assume Jen's role brings a lot of pressure as many carers want change now and the NHS is often in some form of constant change to deal with the challenges of health benefits for all. With the coronavirus, as never before, the world's countries have looked towards their own health systems to cope with this new virus.

The NHS must not lose focus on families and carers and this is a huge role for their experience of care lead, a juggling act that I certainly can admire.

Networking with Fellow Carers

As mentioned earlier on in this book when I talk about carers, I am talking about unpaid carers; I am not talking about care workers who work for a care agency. Care workers are paid and have clients while carers are unpaid and care for someone they are related to or emotionally attached to.

Caring for someone can be extremely isolating. If a carer is spending so much time caring and not networking, they can lose out on support, information and that special carer identity. It is so important to get out there and mingle with like-minded carers.

If you are caring for someone, even if they are not suffering mental illness, then this chapter will give you some ideas as to why networking with carers is important.

Why is Carer Networking so important?

So the big question is why is carer networking important? Why should you as a carer go out there and form networks with other carers?

Consider the following. One of the worst things is for carers to experience isolation. I have been through this in my early years as a carer. I did not know I was isolated and although I was not completely lonely, I often wondered who else out there was caring for someone with a mental illness.

I did not really know much about carer support groups, but when I eventually attended them, the carer support groups only provided some of the answers. I think because there just was not enough time to form bonds with other carers at the group as some carers took up so much time to tell their story, which caused other carers to fall silent or fall asleep. Perhaps it was how the carer support group was facilitated, but I strongly advocate carers to at least try and join carer support groups.

Still the main point is that carers need to feel they belong. The best way to feel you belong is to be connected to others experiencing what you are going through. In the past I made the mistake of assuming friends would understand what I was going through, but eventually most friends moved on with their lives, but what I did notice is the friends who ended up caring for someone actually understood what I was going through and encouraged me to raise awareness of the carer experience. I am not saying that all carers have other carers' interests in mind, but I do feel carers have that common theme in that …. they just get it.

As a carer you do not have to feel a carers' support group is the only way to network with like-minded carers. There are different ways of networking including carer forums, peer networks, AGMs, online forums or even picking up the phone and checking in on a fellow carer.

Carer networking is a way to meet other carers, to exchange ideas, support each other and raise issues. This can be a great way for veteran carers to help educate those new to the caring role and guide them through the pitfalls of the experience of care. I have developed many ways of connecting with carers, although it has not been easy because it can be difficult to find a room or find a place to book group gatherings.

I have been very lucky to be supported by the local carer centres, although if you are a carer without a carer centre, then certainly work into developing a carer group. Expect it to be slightly difficult because you may have to ask others to support you with carers or even find support through social prescribing or community groups.

Eventually the carer network will grow and the bigger the network, the more support carers can get. With these networks they can eventually form links and develop a larger carer movement from an army of millions of carers. This was something I learned from Karen Machin who is a carer peer network champion.

I am not saying that is your task, because I am sure you are busy providing care to someone, but certainly bear in mind that connecting to others sharing your identity is a must.

A big reason to network with carers is that carer's voices should help shape health and social care services. As a network or group, each carer can chip in to find out what is working and what is not. The larger the carer's group then the more ideas that can be formed in to shaping services.

Another good reason for forming networks is that few people pay attention to that one carer's voice, but when it's a dozen, hundreds or more carers making noises then people begin to sit up and notice.

If you are suffering as a carer, then who else out there is going through what you are experiencing?

Other advantages of carer networking

Without information, it is hard to know what your rights are as a carer. Information is usually accessible to carers, but be aware information can become out of date. When networking with other carers there is always a chance you can get up to date information, especially at carer support groups.

You may already know a lot about getting support for yourself; you can always help other carers at meetings or support groups.

Meeting up with other carers need not be a chore, it only takes a few dedicated carers to form a group together and discuss issues which are common in their role. No carer should end up being isolated and carers should not wait for services to respond in order to help them. It is vital carers seek out support groups and carer forums to raise issues and network.

The problems of not networking with carers

If no networking takes place, it's harder to organise if things go wrong. If a large number of carers fail to organise themselves into a group or attend any carer support group, then services may decide to guess what support carers need and then there is a risk services can go wrong. Even worse services might not wish to fund or support carer networks because they feel there is no need for them.

Carers must be vocal about what services affect them and the person they care for.

We cannot always depend on services to support carer's issues.

This might sound harsh, but the NHS and social care system is under immense strain; with years of austerity and the coronavirus pandemic, the system has reached breaking point. Just looking closely at the numbers of people who have passed away in the UK from the coronavirus is a telling sign. Not to say that those battling in health and social care are not working their hardest, it is just the resources and planning did not hit their mark.

Service provision and support need to hear carers' voices, but they can only do half of the work. Health commissioners and mental health staff can only form or create events and groups, if no carer turns up, then service providers will second guess what carers need. Carers should not be naive about services getting things right all the time, although carers should also avoid being negative all the time. As carers we need to link and try to support each other through this challenging coronavirus pandemic.

Types of Carer networking

It does not hurt to remind ourselves about the ways carers can network; below are forms of carer networking that I have found useful in the past.

Carer support groups

These were the first form of groups I attended when I started out on my carer's journey. I was referred to them by my local carers' centre. When I first attended them, I must admit I was scared out of my wits. I was embarrassed to tell others about my carer experience, but over time I began to feel proud that I was supporting someone so close to me.

Carer support groups are great for meeting other carers, but take note that since carer groups can be facilitated then it can be harder to chat to the carer next to you; but they are a start to meeting other carers. One other thing to mention is that not all carer groups are alike, some carer support groups are peer driven and others are led by a trained professional maybe from an NHS trust or a carer support officer runs them. Some carer groups are very relaxed, while others follow a strict format.

The carer support groups I currently run are semi-relaxed as I try and give carers a chance not only to update the group, but I also encourage carers to support others in a welcoming format.

Carer Forums

These kinds of carer groups are not support groups and follow an even stricter format. Forums usually have an agenda of speakers updating members and forums can be closed to members or open to carers and even the public. There is not much time for carers to tell their story because many questions and queries are aimed at the speakers' presentations. A good example of types of speakers at such forums are an NHS mental health professional, someone in charge of carer complaints, member of parliament or a carer lead updating carers on services.

It is often not easy to get engagement from NHS professionals; perhaps because they are rushed off their feet, but if you are lucky enough to have one attend your group, then that is a great sign of a good relationship.

I have heard from some carers that NHS professionals have no business coming to carers groups because it could put carers at risk, but if the group is run well and everyone has good intentions then we can all work towards a health system that cares for the carer. I want everyone to be involved just as if it was a triangle, like the triangle of care policy.

Ringing up known carers.

If you can have an agreement with a carer to contact them, then this can be a form of working towards peer support. Support from carer centre is great when staff is available, but this cannot be 24 hours and I have always pointed out that the bigger the support network, the better the outcomes for everyone.

From the carer support groups I run, I have always tried to make myself available to be a listening ear if a carer is in a desperate situation. There will be a time I will double check with the carer by calling them. Doing such roles can be challenging, especially if you are also caring because our energies are not limitless.

You would need to be careful not to take too much on, but do not let that fully put you off. There was many times when another carer listened to my worries at night and that really made so much difference to me. As long as the carer can keep things in confidence and not try to be pretentious or negative then a good network can form.

Carers need to look out for each other; this is the meaning of being a carer.

Attending carer awareness events.

This is one of the best type of carer networking you can get, especially if the event is aimed at carers. The problem is finding one that is running in your area. You usually get these types of events on awareness days like Carers rights day, or Carer's awareness week or even Young carer's awareness day. If you want to form a network then certainly try attending such events or better yet, try plan your own.

Attending mental health events

This is specific to mental health carers. There might be a chance of attending a mental health event especially during mental health awareness days. Here are some examples:

- Suicide Prevention Day
- Eating Disorders Awareness Week
- World Mental Health Day
- World Bipolar Day
- Mental Health Awareness week

There are lots more awareness events and usually mental health survivors attend these, but the odd carer can also be found attending to find out more about the illness of the person they are caring for.

Signing up to online carer forums

Out of all the carer networking events and tips, this is probably one of the easiest. Carers UK have an online carers' forum, which I use every now and then, but I do not post as much as I used to. Online forums are a great way to find help and support without leaving home and you can even network with carers.

Since so many things are going online especially due to the coronavirus, you do not have to travel and can safely chat at home. The problem is online engagement does not beat meeting someone face to face with a cup of tea, but then again, this form of support is used differently. Plus I have of heard carer groups doing online virtual cuppas.

Carers UK and other charities AGMs

In the past I have really enjoyed Annual General Meetings. One of the biggest is the Carers UK conference because obviously it covers the country, although kept to a format where you can not only meet other carers, but find out the important updates regarding carer's rights and policies. This is perfect if you want to find out more on the carer movement.

There are plenty of other AGMs focusing on carers, even local carer centres have them and it is worth attending; you do not have to go just to meet other carers. You can attend to find out how the organisation is performing.

Attending NHS trust events

I think these are a great way to network with other carers. I am talking about mental health trust carer listening events. I have attended the South London & Maudsley's carers listening day usually held close to carers' awareness week. You get to meet fellow carers from your local mental health trust and because such events can run for several hours, there is plenty of time to chat with fellow carers.

If you're lucky you can even help plan your local mental health trust's carers conference or event. For SLaM, short for South London & Maudsley, they would do the following:

- Update carers on their mental health strategy
- Have a carer tell their story
- A talk by the trust's CEO
- Presentations on how mental health wards are working to be carer friendly
- Break off rooms to learn about Carers rights, carer support or wellbeing
- A chance to visit stalls held by carer centres
- A large lunch provided by the NHS Trust
- A panel where the CEO and others are asked questions by the audience.

I have helped plan such carer events in the past and even spoken at several of them. If you are caring for someone using the services of a mental health trust, certainly ask when they plan to hold their carers' conference. During coronavirus this might be challenging, but with virtual platforms, not impossible.

Attending external carer forums

This one is a tricky one, but not impossible. I have always told carers to venture out and see how other carers are networking. When I mean venture out, I am talking several boroughs away or even to another mental health trust or other carer centre. I mean how can a carer know they are getting the best carer support if they are not comparing or taking notes?

I have always found most carers from other areas very welcoming to outsiders; they probe visitors to their groups about news regarding carer services in their own area. Some carers' eyes pop out of their head if they notice I have travelled far to meet them and it feels me with pride when we compare notes and ideas.

There only have been a few times when confidentiality has blocked me from networking with other carer groups, but if carers cannot connect with each other then it can be difficult to learn from each other. I do admit sometimes carer services can be very protective when they see an unknown carer activist poke their nose through the door. Maybe if the services were in a bad way I can understand, but for carers to be given the chance to learn and be empowered then carers must learn to connect.

Including unpaid carers in NHS Co-Production

I have been in co-production in the NHS for close to 15 years and I still struggle with the concept; when people think of co-production they often tend to focus on those who receive the service. Thus the patient tends to be the focus of engagement. This is not a bad thing, but we must remember not all services are alike and in the NHS there are levels of services that the unpaid carer needs to access.

We also must remember that mental health services cannot risk blocking out those who support the patient/service user. It is common sense that the more people included in the support of the patient, the better the outcomes, despite odd voices that feel carers/families should not be included because they lack the understanding or experience of mental health. Otherwise mental health stigma would continue and create other stigma in the process.

There are many reasons why families and carers need to fight for their equal share in co-production, engagement and inclusion, but that is a book for another time.

Before I continue, co-production is a vast and complex method, so one simple chapter cannot do it justice, so I will revisit this in the future.

Why co-production is needed for carers in the NHS

The NHS is always changing and yet it is almost always the same. Sounds confusing, doesn't it? Technology, new nursing techniques and policies move the NHS forward, yet the NHS focuses on health for all and fights to stay that way. Families and carers although not using the core mental health services, have a vast amount of knowledge in regards to how services can empower everyone. Particularly when the person they care for is using the mental health services. No one wants to take away the power from service users/patients, but power and decisions should try to be shared to include all, especially families and carers.

You do not have to look very hard to find out what happens when families and carers are not listened to. Mental health NHS trusts and their hospitals and services can come under scrutiny when serious incidents occur. Dig down hard enough and you will find a voice warning staff of 'cared for' health concerns. Of course, each scenario should be dealt with in a case by case way, not all carers are angels, but it would be foolish to state the majority of families and carers do not have the 'cared for's' best interests in mind.

Families and carers do not want to take power away from the patients who use the services, in fact they would rather not get involved, simply because there is no time and they would happily just want to get on with their lives. Alas the state of declining services (not just NHS) is a call to arms, not just to plead to the NHS to include families and carers, but for families and carers to sit up and be noticed.

Carers included!!

As a reminder, this chapter is about co-production to include unpaid carers. Unpaid carers are emotionally tied to the 'cared for', be it families, friends or neighbours, but usually it is the families or those in the family unit that fight hard for the 'cared for'.

In no way do I want to push aside the patient/service user, nor do I want to lessen the value of their experience, but if it is hard for the service user to access co-production, then culture might make it very difficult for the family and carer who by numbers alone are lacking in involvement in the NHS at all levels.

Local organisations included

As an unpaid carer, I have been lucky to engage and be involved in a number of organisations, some local and others not so local. I am talking about Carer Centres, local Healthwatch and mental health advocacy/charity organisations. We all know that it is very difficult for the NHS to shape services based on the few, so they have to rely on the third sector to also be the voice for carers. I say 'also' because families and unpaid carers still should be included. Without the support of the organisations, then there are certain risks that can cause co-production to fail.

This could be

- Word not getting out to other unpaid carers to co-produce
- No one knowing what is going on
- Hard to develop services for the community because only the few are listened to
- Relationships break down with the organisations
- Trust begins to break down
- Quality of services deteriorating
- Culture of non-inclusion develops
- Supporting others in their community.

If someone from a clinical back ground is reading this, I am sure they may have got into their profession because they want to support people's health with their skills. It would be difficult to always be around the patient, so due to lack of resources and time, we need to give the skills and power for people to support themselves in their community.

If the power is shared to others to help shape their own health in the community, then resources can avoid extra strain. We want people to value their own health and well-being, to do this we must educate others about the importance of health and educate ourselves on what others think about their own health and the level of services.

It goes without saying the more people are supported to do this, the more it filters down in the community for others to learn from those who are empowered. It is a numbers game, we need to reach out to the majority, even if starting out with the few who push to connect with others. The network should be supported to spread the message.

A Call to arms

The NHS is boring. There!! I said it!! I do not mean any disrespect, but what do I mean when I say this? Sometimes people do not rush to be involved because they cannot understand the dry jargon of the NHS. If it becomes too complex, it then becomes boring. If co-production and inclusion becomes boring, then people keep away, patients keep away and unpaid carers just do not have the time.

Families and carers have enough to worry about, I should know. There is not a day when I am not thinking to myself about the past mistakes, regrets and worries about those I supported and cared for. I often think to myself, why am I in a certain meeting which I clearly do not understand?

Perhaps there needs to be a way where we need to produce exciting initiatives to include families and carers. Is the NHS speaking the language of the service user? Or the language of themselves e.g. NHS jargon? How can we speak the language of families and carers? Of course, the NHS cannot shoulder the blame for everything, sometimes carers can be at fault for being naive about how services are being designed to include them.

Making it as simple as possible

Due to what was mentioned above, it is difficult for the NHS to include those who find interaction and co-production boring. It helps if the NHS can make things as simple as possible. I have seen quite a lot of material and strategy that works this way and I have seen some amazing success stories. Still there are many services that need to focus on what NHS leaflets they are producing. It is not just media or information; it is engagement, inclusion, documents, how meetings are run and organised, and even training.

Investment in people

When you invest in people, it will eventually pay off. Unfortunately, the NHS has a habit of investing in services; there can be a problem of looking at services alone via the cost. This is due to the culture of NHS service commissioning. No fault of the NHS, but there is a tug of war to state we should not just look at the quality of service, invest in the people who the services are being designed for. Investing in people might mean funding their projects, valuing their time, buying in those who can set an example and lead people to be included. It is not always about money either, investment can also mean time and dedication, but we need to invest to value the use of co-production.

How to get people excited?

Maybe it is the language used? People do not all speak the NHS lingo, even though the NHS shapes so many of our lives. We need to get people excited to join in on the co-production. What can the NHS and social services do to learn from others? How do political parties get their voters to vote? How do movie makers get people to watch their films? How do restaurants get people to buy their food? Is it about the product? It is about getting the message across. Health is important to us all, but how can we get families and carers to be excited about this? We do not always need to have the angry carer screaming for co-production. It should also be about carers wanting to make a change and a difference.

Carers plunging into to co-production can sometimes get it wrong, but doing so will be an example to others. Carers have to try and answer the call.

Same old problems

Did I mention the NHS has a culture of being the same? There have been some important meetings where I am hearing from service users that the NHS tends to reward itself. We hear the same stories of influences being rewarded (usually the top awards) in the NHS all being NHS CEOs? There might be the odd service user or carer. Take a look at some NHS trusts' twitter feeds to see how some trusts can be rather self-serving. This is not a major criticism since it is important to value hard working staff, but you often wonder why patients and carers are not mentioned in regards to their successes?

Alongside getting people excited for co-production to happen, there should also be initiatives as well. We want to reward those who lead by example. This is because leading by example can be hard work and those leaders are the first to make mistakes, because they are the first to try.

If you want co-production to spread, we have to show how it is valued on the hospital wards, the community services and beyond. We cannot just include others and then tell them 'thank you' and get lost. We need to value their time and reward them, but how?

What are we getting out of this?

It is a 'no brainer' this one. The first thing to change would be that service quality would improve. Next would be culture change, which is hard to change by itself. People would care about the NHS services, and I mean not the few, but the many. We would have a filter down process where people would speak more about the services as they would speak about what was on TV last night.

Staff would not have to feel so much pressure as there would be more confidence to provide the service people want. Of course, we have to be realistic; we cannot design services to make everyone happy. There will be that person who is unhappy about everything and would want change now, but that is not possible and such people will find themselves being shut out.

We want unpaid carers to be self-sufficient where they are empowered to be so. We want families and carers to be included and be excited about being included. We want a culture change to reward and value those who want to see change.

The coronavirus battle by the NHS front line did cause others to appreciate the work the NHS has been doing, especially with the 'clap for our carers' campaign. It however would be a big mistake if people decided a clap is all that is needed. The public must work to understand the NHS, test the NHS, hold it to account and get involved, especially when it comes to their health. The coronavirus is a great tester of health and social care systems. It tested the UK and we all know the result, we must now work to care for the health system, or how can it care for us?

Standing on the shoulders of giants

I am sure co-production sprung out of the service user movement. There must be many examples out there, especially due to the mistakes psychiatry made in the past such as the persecution of LGBT groups, institutionalisation, misunderstanding and high death rates of BAME patients, problems of being quick to label others mentally unwell due to new diagnosis and so on. I will not pretend I know everything about co-production and I should not be celebrated for doing so. However, I will admit that we all can and should contribute to co-production; even if it fails, it still sets an example to the next generation.

The stigma of an unpaid Mental Health Carer

I find it quite important that you must not forget the hidden heroes who carry on when their loved ones are in most need. This is not to take away the difficult battles mental health survivors face, however all too often stigma hits out at more than one person.

Mental health stigma hits the family, the friend, the husband, the wife and even the neighbour. This chapter will concentrate on another type of stigma, which can be all too well forgotten. I am going to talk about carer stigma. Now it is very important that not all unpaid carers suffer from carer stigma.

First you must differentiate what or who is an unpaid carer. I am talking about the person who suddenly finds themselves caring for someone close to them who has been unfortunate to pick up either physical or mental health problems. I am not talking about paid care workers; although I do admit care workers find they can have a difficult job, they are paid for their role and can be protected by the Union.

With carers, they are not trained and often care out of closeness and love for the person they are trying to look out for. It gets really difficult if that person has a mental health illness.

The types of carer stigma

I cannot really produce an exhaustive list of different types of carer stigma, but the ones that I am showing will probably the most recognisable types in carers' lives out there.

Depends on the illness

When a loved one becomes very unwell, the carer often tries as hard as they can to support them. The problem is the more chronic the illness the more stigma lashes out. A good example is when a carer is caring for someone suffering psychosis; those suffering from this difficult illness can often present challenging behaviours. If such behaviour is out in public, then the challenge is not only faced by the mental health survivor but also the carer.

It only takes one person to ridicule the suffering from a mental health problem. This can then extend to the person's family; the risk is once a community starts to gossip about the situation, it can cause the carer and patient to become more isolated. This in turn leads to stigma of both mental health and carer. As a note, not all carers go through this and it probably can depend upon the illness anyway.

The Label

Although not as devastating as the first form of carer stigma, it still can be rather destructive. Some people carry on caring and supporting those close to them out of desperation. They carry on caring regardless of the support mechanisms that may not be applied to the family network.

At first it seemed really brave; it is great to hear a carer battle it out no matter what the situation. However, there is one big problem: no matter what the carers might say to this situation, the person still feels that they do not deserve the term of being labelled a carer. The problem is that this person will then likely not access the support network available for carers.

Clashing forms of relations

This type of stigma is actually quite similar to the one mentioned previously. A good example is when a person marries someone, they marry for better or worse. When the worst does arrive, the person cares especially out of love. They care because they are either the husband or wife. If you try to tell them that they are now a carer, that person may become very irritated. They refuse to be labelled as a carer, and yes this is their right, but the risk is a lack of support network available to them.

This carer stigma can also extend to other relations within the family; another good example is a young person caring for a parent, or even especially a young carer. Can you imagine as a child having to suddenly provide care for an older adult suffering a mental health condition?

The terrible characteristics of an unpaid mental health carer

There are several characteristics, which are aimed at carers. I am going to go through a few that come off the top of my head.

Being labelled as lazy

All too often we have to work for a living; we have to pay our dues. The harder the work we do, the more we expect to be paid. The more complex the role, the more we expect be rewarded. There is this view going around that the caring role is fairly easy, because some people think that it is easy, they think that the carer does not have to do much at all. This can lead to carers being labelled as lazy. Once a person is targeted as lazy, they do not really want to be labelled as a carer.

Being blamed

This is quite common in the field of psychology/psychiatry, especially in America. When someone is unfortunate enough to develop a mental health problem, all too often psychiatrists tend to probe the family structure. All too often, it says the carer is not doing their job properly. It might even go so far as to state that the carer is causing the mental health relapse or has caused the mental health problem to manifest itself in the first place.

One of the main criticisms of psychiatry is at one end it might exclude the carer in their supporting role/care plans or confidentiality and at the other end label the carer as the problem within care plans and assessments. This can lead to a person not really wanting to find the energy to battle the mental health system that can misunderstand the caring role.

Confrontational

Another good example of how the mental health system might fail families and carers, is if the carer has experienced failures in support of their loved ones and even the care of their own self. It then becomes only a matter of time before the carer becomes more confrontational. No one really wants to be labelled as aggressive, uncooperative and confrontational. This is just another label a person can do without, so why would they want to be labelled as a carer?

Risk of declining health

Again this might depend upon the type of illness the person is trying to care for, the more chronic the illness, the most stressful the situation is for the carer. Since the NHS is under severe strain, a person would have to think hard and long before they would want to commit themselves in becoming an unpaid carer. It is like there has been a secret contract, stating that the carer now must take the role of the missing staff within the health system. This could be administering medication, advocating, understanding side effects, understanding social welfare, mental health legal matters, engaging with doctors, as well as mental health advocate and peer supporter roles.

Is there any wonder why carers can end up with depression, anxiety, stress and worry? One could say that mental illness can be catching.

Hiding it all away

I'm afraid I have bad news, for what I have mentioned is only the tip of the iceberg when it comes to carer stigma. I did not want to make this chapter overly long, but give a little taste of what stigma can be like. With the above issues, is it any wonder why someone wants to hide themselves from being labelled as a carer?

What I learned as a carer

Over my caring journey, I have learned so much. Some of the things I have learned from experience, while other knowledge was taught. Each moment I look back on my life lessons, I feel grateful to have gone through them. I do sometimes regret the mistakes and wonder what I could have done differently, but in the end all I can do is be human and humans are made to make those mistakes.

In this this chapter I have listed out what I have learned though my journey caring for my mother.

I am a carer

Without a doubt this is the most important thing I have learned. Early on when caring for my mother, I would think I am just doing my duty and out of love for my mother, but after a while when attending my local carer centre, I found out I was providing an important role as a carer.

I did not know what my role was, or what my carer's rights were. If you are caring for someone, it is so important to identify as a carer. Even if you do not get anything out of it, the role can help with your identity.

Stronger sense of purpose

Only near the end of my carer journey did I find this out. It is not something that is instant, and takes time to form over a long period of time. I did so much for my mother and the family, but those caring attributes can be transferred on to other things. I once did an online course from Carers UK called "Learning for Living" and it shows carers can pick up many skills when they are providing care; the course also helped in planning for the future.

Still a stronger sense of purpose in life is more than just skill forming. As a carer you experience how harsh things can become for the family. You see the frailty of human life, you also see how important community is and why we must all do our bit. If you are caring for someone, you are showing others how important it is to be there, you are setting an example to the community and in turn the community can become a caring one.

My purpose is to set an example that caring for those close to you is a sign of a civilised society, where we deal with the stigma of physical and mental health and look out for each other.

Proud to have fought the battle to the very end

Very few people want the life of the person they care for to end. People care because they want to improve the quality of someone's life. When someone they love passes away, a lot of carers feel guilty and they feel that they failed. I should know because I have experienced this. When my mother passed away after so many years, I often wondered to myself what could I have done differently?

Maybe I should have pushed harder and knocked down doors to help my mother out? I do not know and I guess I never will know, but the other side of the coin is that I never gave up. I can at least say I was there till the bitter end, to the point where my journey has taken a new path. I have experienced the grief and loss of losing someone close and can share this with former carers. It is very hard to know what it's like until you have experienced such a difficult event, but I am so glad that I helped my mother the best I could. I now need to try care for myself.

Setting an example to others

This is a thing carers do not know until later on in their caring journeys. Whatever we do, we are always setting an example to other people. It could be the way we act or how we talk, but when advocating the importance of providing care then it is setting an example. I wish to carry on setting an example to others especially during this coronavirus pandemic.

More people will end up broken from the outcome of the virus. Some will lose everything including their mental health, which means people will have to taking on a caring role. It could be your father who has lost his job, your sister who lost her husband due to the virus.

It could be depressing situations which trigger mental health isssues, and even surviving the virus can sometimes cause lasting physical and mental effects, especially for those whose life was on the line and somehow pulled through after catching the virus. With all the above mentioned, it shows we need to be a caring society and a lot more will be expected of us. I am not saying it will be easy, but I know many out there would not want someone close to them suffer and they will take on a caring role.

The strength of family

When I was young I never really thought much about family, I just did what I was told and assumed my family identity. It is only when tragedy strikes the family that the strength of family shines through. Caring for someone in the family shows that the family structure still exists. I have learned that I have done much in the name of being a family member.

I kept family bonds as much as possible and I will continue to be a part of the family to my brothers and sister. I am sure there will be errors and I am sure there will be a time I may have to care again, but when things get tough I will show I care about the family and family should come first.

I have been worn down

Caring for someone can bring many rewards, for example what I have mentioned in this chapter on reflecting on what I have learned. Still it is so important to note that over the years caring has worn me down. I have fought really hard to deal with mental health issues when going through really difficult times as a carer. Some people say mental illness can only really affect those who are suffering from it, but I do not see it as a black and white issue. Stress, depression and anxiety can all be mental health issues if experienced for very long periods. All these symptoms can be experienced by carers, not to say carers get the worst of it, but it does show mental health issues can be catching.

So over the years I have not gone through unscathed. There are times when I pause and zone out thinking about traumatic experiences when I used to hear my mother scream at night when she was battling nightmares her mental illness was throwing at her.

I was worn down by her distrust of me thinking I was trying to harm her and cause her life misery and pain when I had to intervene when her health was at risk. There were financial worries of dealing with debt when my mother struggled with financial problems; I often wondered how we would survive as loans and debts were piling up and few were concerned about her mental illness. Worst of all when I was really down, some in the community thought it funny to see someone depressed, but many were very supportive of what I was trying to do and that gave me hope. There are some very good people out there.

Had to sacrifice a lot

I learned that I had to put a lot on the line. It might sound mean, but many carers have to put careers on hold. Some avoid relationships and even if they do take on a partner then the risk is the partner would be dismissive or pressure the carer to leave their role. I lost a lot of friends who did not have time for me, but I did make comrades with other carers who knew how tough the role was.

It is so important to learn what you are sacrificing, not to make others feel guilty, but to see what can help out in the future or what could replace the loss. It is like trying to plan for the future. Many carers make the ultimate sacrifice as when their loved one passes away, the carer suffers because they have not invested time in other skills, have no one around to care for them and some carers can even lose their home. Sacrifice is common and time usually is the first thing to be sacrificed.

My story must mean something

With writing this very book and with many other mental health carers out there, my story must mean something to someone. I have been through a difficult caring journey, but I have left signs, tracks and made a path for others to follow. When you go through a journey, then it is easier to look back and guide others. I will never tire of telling my story and hope it can be a lesson for other carers, health professionals or social workers.

If you are caring, then never feel your story is the same as everyone else as "No carers journey is the same". We all are unique in what we experience even if we are labelled in the same role.

Many battles to fight

Just because my role as a mental health carer has finished, it does not mean I can sit back and not use my skills to make a difference. I have seen so many things as carer that I wish to change. It could be issues and challenges with health and social care. The battles could be in encouraging carers to stand together and use their voice to make a difference.

There are many battles to fight and I will stand strong with other carers because I have worn that badge. I will of course make mistakes, but I often tell other carers we need to try and get better support for unpaid carers. There will be those that disagree with what carers face and that's ok as we all have our opinions, but as it stands unpaid carers, especially young carers still struggle in the community.

Developing a caring community

Talking about community it might be the second most used word after caring. One of the reasons I developed a lot of carer groups and forums was for a strong sense of community. I feel that community is a shared sense of belonging and values. We all have come from some family and many will go on to form families. With families they all belong to a community and a good community will tie people together and support them.

If I am caring for someone close and others learn from that, I hope they will care and support each other, which will lead to a caring community. What is wrong with wanting that? Is it any wonder that so many people suffer mental ill health and isolation because the community was fragmented and did not care?

As mentioned before, we all set an example in what we say or how we act. As a carer I have learned that I have been trying to connect to the community and hope it can become a caring one, because one day I am counting on that community to care for me.

Printed in Great Britain
by Amazon